Great Grilles of the '50s

Mark Misercola   Hank Kaczmarek

M.T. Publishing Company, Inc.™

P.O. Box 6802, Evansville, Indiana 47719-6802
www.mtpublishing.com

Library of Congress Control Number:
2019943990

ISBN: 978-1-949478-25-9
Design and Pre-press by
Alena L. Kiefer, M.T. Publishing Company, Inc.™

Printed in the United States of America.

This 1953 Fiesta, which graces the front cover of this book, was restored by Mike Fusick, owner of Fusick Automotive Inc., in East Windsor, Connecticut.

Contents

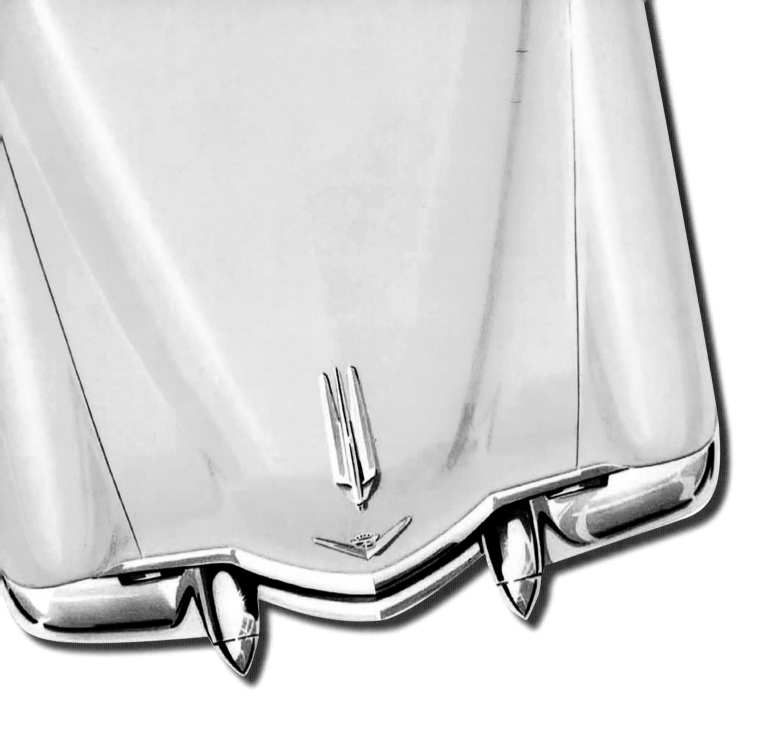

Introduction

The 1950s was a "golden era" for Detroit, reflecting the endless optimism and futuristic view in America following World War II. Car designers and stylists were inspired by current-day fighter jets, space age technology and chrome. Their creations sported shiny chrome grilles, bullet-nosed bumpers, enormous tail fins, cockpit-styled dashboards, and frames as big as aircraft carriers. Many have called them art work on wheels. The allure and emotional appeal of these cars has been well-documented in countless books over the years. But, without exception, all of these titles look at fabulous '50s vehicles as the sum of their parts. None focus specifically on what many consider to be the most distinguishing aspect of many of these vehicles – their amazing front grilles.

Great Grilles of the '50s provides a close-up view, both visually and in narrative form, of the best and most dynamic grilles of the era. Every grille has a unique story behind it. For example, contrary to conventional wisdom the bullet nose "Dagmar Bumpers" that graced the front ends of many Cadillacs and other models of the day, were not inspired by the popular buxom television actress with the same name. The conical-shaped bumper guards were originally conceived by Harley Earl, GM's legendary vice president of design, to mimic artillery shells and were intended to protect the vehicles' front ends in collisions. In one sense, they were an early-warning, bumper-protection system.

Another example involves the dramatic wide oval grille on the 1957 Chevy, which was created as part of a frantic development program to rush the car to market in response to the public's less than enthusiastic reaction to the Ferrari-inspired grille on the 1955 Chevrolets. When it was done, Chevy had a masterpiece. But many of the designers who worked on the '57's development at the time hated the grille and doubted consumers would ever embrace it. Fortunately for Chevy, history proved them wrong.

We've had a blast putting this book together. The real challenge wasn't so much in writing the book or chasing the photos, it was in narrowing down the selection to those featured here. Our list is by no means exhaustive; it is merely our subjective selection of what we consider the best that Detroit had to offer during the fabulous '50s.

We hope you enjoy reading about them as much as we enjoyed writing about them.

Here's to great grilling!

Chapter 1
1953 Packard Caribbean: Grilled to Perfection

That Packard Smile: The 1953 Packard Caribbean Convertible's front grille was considered the essence of understated elegance, and it connected with consumers in a big way. This production model is owned by Stuart Blond, editor of the Packard Club's *Cormorant Magazine*, who supplied the factory photo.

Like fashion, automotive design underwent a dramatic transformation following World War II. The days of high riding sedans were over, as American roads improved (negating the need for greater clearance between the bottom of the car and the road). At the same time, men's high-topped fedoras gradually went out of fashion, so there was no need for all that extra headroom and ultra-high headliners in the passenger compartment.

By the early 1950s, American cars had become lower, sleeker and more balanced proportionately. Detroit's designers were taking their visual cues (and inspiration) from the wings and tails of American fighter aircraft. The stately vertical "waterfall" grilles that dominated early automotive designs of the 1920s, '30s and '40s gradually were replaced by chrome-laden horizontal grilles that gave each brand distinctive personalities of their own.

Packard emerged from the war lagging behind Cadillac as the automotive world's styling leader. The company's pre-war designs were considered old and dated, and American consumers regarded Packards as "old man's cars."

So, in 1951, Packard's entire lineup got a makeover, and two years later, the Packard Caribbean debuted as a replacement for the venerable Packard Super 8 Series, which was produced from 1939 to 1951.

Packard desperately needed a sporty and sleek option for its lineup, and in 1952 created a show car only convertible model called the Pan American. Henney Auto Body, which collaborated with Packard and built many famous custom Packard models over the years, called the Pan American "the first truly American sports car." This concept served as the base for the Caribbean, and the Pan American grille features were used with only a few minor changes for the production vehicle.

Instead of creating a new body platform, Packard picked the body from its Cavalier model, and sent it to coach builder Mitchell-Bentley for the necessary modifications. There were no modifications to the grille, but a large scoop was added to the hood. The remainder of the front end looks exactly as it was portrayed in the Pan-American concept car.

When compared to some of the more excessive chrome grilles of the late '50s, the Caribbean's wrap-around design is the essence of understated elegance, and one of our top picks for grilles from the decade.

Photo: Antique Automobile Club of America

The Caribbean's headlights, which were mounted high in the front fender peaks, and transverse grille bars made the car appear as if it was smiling. Compared to the frowning grilles that graced many competitive GM models at the time, the Caribbean's struck a responsive chord with consumers.

It is also likely that the American Automobile Association used the Caribbean's grille as a model when designing the "Otto the Auto" talking car in its informational cartoons for children in the 1950s-60s.

GM and Ford noticed. If you look closely at many of their mid-'50s offerings, you will find the same friendly styling smiling right back at you.

The Caribbean's Pan-American heritage was no big secret back in the day. In fact, a *Hemmings Motor News* report states that a prototype Caribbean was painted in a light shade of metallic green as "a kind of tribute to the Pan American, which itself was painted in a color called 'green-gold.' This was a play on the slang Latin American term for Americans, 'gringo' – and it made a slight return in theme as Mopar 'Green-go' in the 1970s."

Packard also showcased both cars in a joint New Year's Day appearance in the Tournament of Roses Parade in Pasadena, Calif., shortly after they debuted.

"There's no question it was a beautiful, well-balanced car and it started at the front," said Ralph Marano, a noted Packard collector and classic car dealer from New Jersey. "I've always considered Packards more than rolling sculptures, they're pieces of American history. And the Caribbean is certainly part of that."

In the end, Marano notes, neither the Pan American nor the Caribbean, or the introduction of its overhead valve V-8 engine in 1955, were enough to counter the mid-range competitive threats that Packard faced from GM, Ford and Chrysler.

"Packard was going up against more than Cadillac," he said. "The middle of the lineup was competing against Pontiac, Olds and Buick, and there were just too many models. And then they brought in Jim Nance as president from Maytag. He didn't know anything about selling cars and the merger with Studebaker was a disaster."

The low production of the initial Caribbean was likely due to its sticker price of $5,210 (roughly $49,000 in today's dollars), making it $2,000 more than its Cavalier cousin, and $1,400 more than a comparable Cadillac in 1953. But because so few of the initial Caribbeans were made, it remains a highly desirable collectible. Survivors in original condition or properly restored can command prices in the low six-figure range.

But as we look back at the decade in grilles, there's no question that the first car to make us smile is the 1953 Packard Caribbean.

This photo shows a prototype of the 1953 Caribbean (the Packard logo on the driver fender only appeared on the prototype), owned by Stuart Blond.

"DUCO" STOCK, ORDER AND CODE NUMBER	Color Scheme

1172-H★
202-55H24-H Yosemite Blue Metallic
  245-0594-K Organic Blue   H, BH (L) HT (U)
  246-0484 Brown
  246-0097 White
  246-0785-G Blue-Toned Green
  202-082 Metallic Base (Fine)

★DUCO 1172-H Yosemite Blue Metallic

1355-M
202-57143-M Matadore Maroon, Metallic
  246-0887-M Medium Maroon   U, UM (U), TU (U)
  246-030-R Light Red
  202-081 Metallic Base (Coarse)

DUCO 1355-M Matador Maroon Metallic

1518-H★
260-57370-H Regimental Gray "Metalli-Chrome"
  246-0484 Brown   A, AF (U)
  246-0594-K Organic Blue
  246-0097-White
  246-0312-M Fast Red
  202-081 Metallic Base (Coarse)

★DUCO 1518-H Regimental Gray "Metalli-Chrome"

1519★
202-57371 Meridian Blue Metallic
  246-051 Milori Blue   B, BH (U)
  246-025 Black
  246-0312-M Fast Red
  202-082 Metallic Base (Fine)

★DUCO 1519 Meridian Blue Metallic

1520★
246-57372 Polaris Blue
  246-0097 White   C
  246-0751-G Chrome Oxide Green
  246-025 Black
  246-0594K Organic Blue

★DUCO 1520 Polis Blue

1521★
202-57373 Dresden Gray Metallic
  246-0097 White   F, AF (L), XF (L)
  246-0751-G Chrome Oxide Green
  246-064 Ferrite Yellow
  202-082 Metallic Base (Fine)

★DUCO 1521 Dresden Gray Metallic

1522-H★
260-57374-H Galahad Green "Metalli-Chrome"
  246-0484 Brown   K, KO (U)
  246-0785-G Blue-Toned Green
  246-025 Black
  202-081 Metallic Base (Coarse)

★DUCO 1522-H Galahad Green "Metalli-Chrome"

"DUCO" STOCK, ORDER AND CODE NUMBER	Color Scheme

1523★
246-57375 Topeka Tan
  246-0097 White   M. UM (L)
  246-0484 Brown
  246-0312-M Fast Red
  246-025 Black

★DUCO 1523 Topeka Tan

1524★
246-57376 Orchard Green
  246-0097 White   O, KO (L)
  246-0751-G Chrome Oxide Green
  246-064 Ferrite Yellow
  246-025 Black

★DUCO 1524 Orchard Green

1525★
245-57377 Carolina Cream
  246-0097 White   T, HT (L), UT (L), XT (L)
  246-0612-K Green Gold Toner
  246-064 Ferrite Yellow
  246-025 Black

★DUCO 1525 Carolina Cream

★ A Du Pont mixing machine formula for DULUX Enamel is available.

1953 Packard Color Bulletin No. 16, Issued December 31, 1952 (Recreated for this publication for space and readability. *www.packardinfo.com*)

1952 Packard Color Scheme

Combination Number	DUCO Code	Color
A	260-57370-H	Regimental Gray "Metalli-Chrome
B	202-57371	Meridian Blue Metallic
C	246-57372	Polaris Blue
F	202-57373	Dresden Gray Metallic
H	202-55824-H	Yosemite Blue Metallic
K	260-37374-H	Galahad Green "Metalli-Chrome"
M	246-57375	Topeka Tan
O	246-57376	Orchard Green
T	246-57377	Carolina Cream
U	202-57143-M	Matador Maroon Metallic
X	246-20848	Black
Upper AF	260-57370-H	Regimental Gray "Metalli-Chrome
Lower	202-57373	Dresden Gray Metallic
Upper BH	202-57371	Meridian Blue Metallic
Lower	202-55824-H	Yosemite Blue Metallic
Upper HT	202-55824-H	Yosemite Blue Metallic
Lower	246-57377	Carolina Cream
Upper KO	260-57374-H	Galahad Green "Metalic-Chrome"
Lower	246-57376	Orchard Green
Upper UM	202-57143-M	Matador Maroon Metallic
Lower	246-57375	Topeka Tan
Upper UT	202-57143-M	Matador Maroon Metallic
Lower	246-57377	Carolina Cream
Upper XF	246-2048	Black
Lower	202-57373	Dresden Gray Metallic
Upper XT	246-2048	Black
Lower	246-57377	Carolina Cream

Grille Tech Sheet: 1953 Packard Caribbean Convertible

Manufacturer: Packard Motor Co, Detroit MI

Body By: Packard, modified by Mitchell-Bentley, Ionia, MI.
(No relation to future GM Styling Chief Bill Mitchell)

Model #2631 Body/Style # 2678.

1953 model year production: 750 units.

Engine: 327 cubic inch inline 8-Cylinder L Head "Thunderbolt," 180 HP/300 ft. lbs. torque.

Transmission:
3-speed Manual (Standard)
2 speed Ultramatic Automatic Transmission – (available after 1/1/1953)

Curb Weight: 4,290 lbs./1,945 kg.

MSRP: $5210.00 ($49,100 in 2018 dollars)

Current Values by condition from Hagerty:
#1 $104,000
#2 $77,100
#3 $60,500
#4 $32,300

Production Colors: Polaris Blue, Gulf Green Metallic, Maroon Metallic, Sahara Sand. (A handful were special-ordered in Metallic Black and Ivory.)

Upholstery: Leather

Fast Facts

Did you know?

- The 1953 Packard Caribbean (accent on the third syllable) had a limited production run of just 750 vehicles.
- It was one of several limited-run "sports cars" with Latin American names in 1952, which served as the inspiration for the Caribbean, the Balboa in 1953, and the Pacific and Panama in 1954.
- The limited-edition Caribbean was Packard's "halo vehicle" that drew attention to the brand and buyers into showrooms.
- The Caribbean's styling was derived directly from the Packard Cavalier. Mitchell-Bentley Corp. modified standard Packard convertible bodies, to achieve a sleek, elegant European appearance.
- At a time when chrome trims were becoming a dominant styling feature on American cars, the Caribbean stood out because it had no regular side trim, but special full-wheel cutouts and rocker panels edged in chrome.
- The Caribbean is a highly desirable collectible. Survivors in top condition routinely command six-figure prices and many reside in private collections.
- The Caribbean competed at the high end of the market. At $5,200, it was priced more than $1,000 above Cadillac's Series 62 convertible.
- The Caribbean was designed by Dick Teague, a talented young stylist who often was called Packard's "wizard of facelifts." His designs are credited with revitalizing the brand's look following the immediate post-war years, when some Packard's were referred to as "pregnant elephants."

Chapter 2:
A Grille to Remember (or Not): The 1958 Edsel Citation

Perhaps no grille in history has defined or doomed a car more than the Edsel.

Inspired by the 1937 LaSalle's vertically centered, egg crate grille, Edsel's notable nose is considered by many automotive enthusiasts to be the worst design flaw in automotive styling and the biggest marketing fiasco in history, prior to Coca-Cola's ill-fated launch of New Coke in 1985.

To be fair, the public's reaction to the grille (more on that later) wasn't the only thing going against the Edsel when it was introduced in 1958 on the heels of the biggest economic downturn since the end of World War II. The Edsel was pricier than GM's mid-level competitors, when consumers weren't feeling confident enough about the economy (or their job prospects) to shell out more money for a car that many felt wasn't as "remarkable and new" as Ford's advertising had promised.

At the same time, some of the Edsel's more innovative and highly touted features failed to catch on. For example, drivers confused the Edsel's "Teletouch" transmission shifter for turn signal indicators and discovered how challenging a simple right or left-hand turn could be when the car suddenly shifted from drive to reverse.

If that wasn't enough, Edsels were plagued with production defects, courtesy of Ford assembly line employees who didn't want to work on the new model or have anything to do with the Edsel Division's plans.

But the Edsel's grille was definitely at the heart of the firestorm. The look was the brainchild of Edsel Design Studio Chief Stylist Roy Brown, Jr., who started his career with GM, and never denied the influence the 1937 LaSalle had on the Edsel.

"Ford wanted something totally new and different," he said in one interview. "At one time, everyone loved the styling [of the LaSalle] but it was no longer in fashion. So we thought here's something that's so old it will be completely different and new."

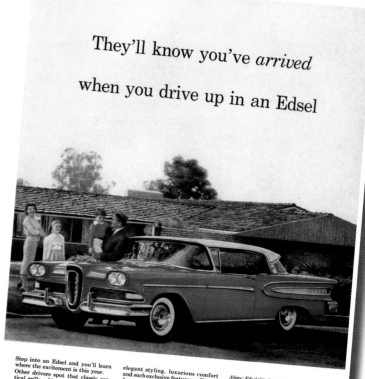

They'll know you've *arrived* when you drive up in an Edsel

Step into an Edsel and you'll learn where the excitement is this year. Other drivers spot that classic vertical grille a block away—and never fail to take a long look at this year's most exciting car.

On the open road, your Edsel is watched eagerly for its already-famous performance.

And parked in front of your home, your Edsel always gets even more attention—because it always says a lot about you. It says you chose elegant styling, luxurious comfort and such exclusive features as Edsel's famous Teletouch Drive—only shift that puts the buttons where they belong, on the steering-wheel hub.

Your Edsel also means you made a wonderful buy. For of all medium-priced cars, this one really new car is actually priced the lowest.* See your Edsel Dealer this week.

*Based on comparison of suggested retail delivered prices of the Edsel Ranger and similarly equipped cars in the medium-price field.

Above: Edsel Citation 2-door Hardtop. Engine: the E-475, with 10.5 to one compression ratio, 345 hp, 475 ft.-lb. torque. Transmission: Automatic with Teletouch Drive. Suspension: Ball-joint with optional air suspension. Brakes: self-adjusting.

EDSEL DIVISION · FORD MOTOR COMPANY

1958 **EDSEL**

Of all medium-priced cars, the one that's really new is the lowest-priced, too!

The public thought differently. It was derided as the "horse collar" grille – in part because of the way it looked and, partially, because of Ford's marketing tie-in with the popular TV western, Wagon Train. The infamous campaign was backed by a nationwide promotional test drive contest that offered free ponies to the winners. The campaign bombed, dealerships were stuck caring for ponies, and many dealers found there was more of a market for selling ponies than the cars.

But Brown wasn't alone in his admiration for the grille design. In a business where many designers and their creations were kept close to the vest, it's surprisingly easy to find the name Jim Sipple listed as the mind behind the "horse collar" grille. His singular design was sometimes described as looking like a part of the female human anatomy, or as an "Oldsmobile sucking on a lemon." The infamous grille was considered

Nose for Bad News: In 1958, there was no shortage of opinions about the front grille of the Edsel Citation (pictured below from a dealer brochure). But time has been much kinder to the Edsel than consumers were in the day.

a major turnoff to men, who as the primary buyers in those days, made their purchase decisions at the dealership.

The "horse collar" grille was considered part of the bumper assembly. The center chrome section is officially known as the "impact ring."

The Edsel lasted only three model years, and the front grille on the 1960 bears little resemblance to the original on the '58. But by then, it was too late to save the Edsel from marketing's hall of shame. It was a costly lesson for Ford. Total Edsel sales were approximately 116,000, less than half the company's projected break-even point. Ford lost $350 million, or the equivalent of more than $2.3 billion by today's standards, on the venture, and the failure influenced the company's plans for years.

Case studies often refer to the Edsel alternatively as the "wrong car at the wrong time," "the flop heard round the world," and "the biggest marketing fiasco of all-time." Time and the collectible car market have softened that view. With 60 years of history in the rear-view mirror, the Edsel's nose is considered by many to be an "iconic" grille. Those who are fortunate enough to own a high-powered, sporty Edsel Citation Convertible are having the last laugh today, particularly if you look at current pricing valuations.

The Edsel Citation 4-Door Hardtop

CITATION

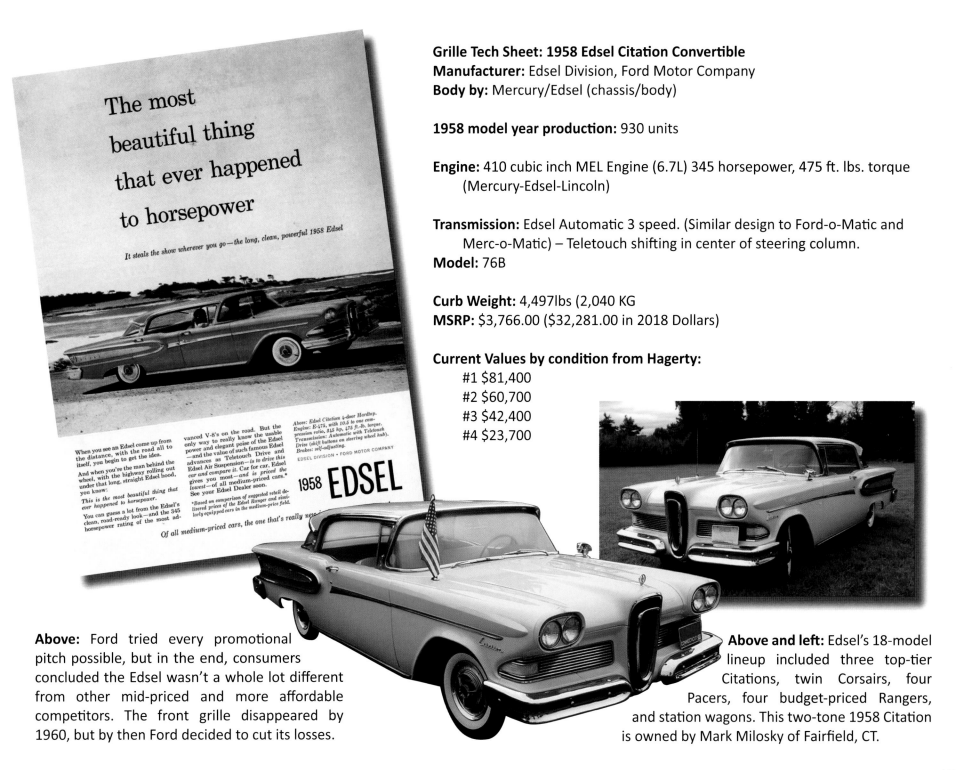

Grille Tech Sheet: 1958 Edsel Citation Convertible
Manufacturer: Edsel Division, Ford Motor Company
Body by: Mercury/Edsel (chassis/body)

1958 model year production: 930 units

Engine: 410 cubic inch MEL Engine (6.7L) 345 horsepower, 475 ft. lbs. torque (Mercury-Edsel-Lincoln)

Transmission: Edsel Automatic 3 speed. (Similar design to Ford-o-Matic and Merc-o-Matic) – Teletouch shifting in center of steering column.
Model: 76B

Curb Weight: 4,497lbs (2,040 KG
MSRP: $3,766.00 ($32,281.00 in 2018 Dollars)

Current Values by condition from Hagerty:
- #1 $81,400
- #2 $60,700
- #3 $42,400
- #4 $23,700

The most beautiful thing that ever happened to horsepower

It steals the show wherever you go—the long, clean, powerful 1958 Edsel

When you see an Edsel come up from the distance, with the road all to itself, you begin to get the idea.

And when you're the man behind the wheel, with the highway rolling out under that long, straight Edsel hood, you know:

This is the most beautiful thing that ever happened to horsepower.

You can guess a lot from the Edsel's clean, road-ready look—and the 345 horsepower rating of the most advanced V-8's on the road. But the only way to really know the usable power and elegant poise of the Edsel —and the value of such famous Edsel advances as Teletouch Drive and Edsel Air Suspension—is to drive this Edsel. Car for car, Edsel car and compare it. Car for car, Edsel gives you most—and is priced the lowest—of all medium-priced cars.*

See your Edsel Dealer soon.

*Based on comparison of suggested retail delivered prices of the Edsel Ranger and similarly equipped cars in the medium-price field.

Above: Edsel Citation 4-door Hardtop.
Engine: E-475, with 10.5 to one compression ratio, 345 hp, 475 ft.-lb. torque. Transmission: Automatic with Teletouch Drive (shift buttons on steering wheel hub). Brakes: self-adjusting.

EDSEL DIVISION • FORD MOTOR COMPANY

1958 **EDSEL**

Of all medium-priced cars, the one that's really new

Above: Ford tried every promotional pitch possible, but in the end, consumers concluded the Edsel wasn't a whole lot different from other mid-priced and more affordable competitors. The front grille disappeared by 1960, but by then Ford decided to cut its losses.

Above and left: Edsel's 18-model lineup included three top-tier Citations, twin Corsairs, four Pacers, four budget-priced Rangers, and station wagons. This two-tone 1958 Citation is owned by Mark Milosky of Fairfield, CT.

1958 Edsel Colors

Ford Paint Code	Merch. Paint Code	Color
B	50	DQE-31589-DAL SILVER GRAY POLY.
C	40	DQE-70794-DAL EMBER RED
D	95	DQE-41991-DAL TURQUOISE
E Ranger Pacer Only		DQE-8103-DAL SNOW WHITE
E Corsair Citation Only		DQE-8150-DAL FROST WHITE.
F	25	DQE-11687-DAL POWDER BLUE
G	26	DQE-11703-DAL HORIZON BLUE
H	27	DQE-11693-DAL ROYAL BLUE.
J	10	DQE-42165-DAL ICE GREEN
K	11	DQE-42164-DAL SPRING GREEN.
L	12	DQE-42168-DAL SPRUCE GREEN POLY.

Ford Paint Code	Merch. Paint Code	Color
M	60	DQE-21469-DAL CHARCOAL BROWN POLY.
N		DQE-31346-DAL DRIFTWOOD
Q	70	DQE-80840-DAL JONQUIL YELLOW
R		DQE-70793-DAL SUNSET CORAL
T	85	DQE-70632-DAL CHALK PINK.
U	80	DQE-21473-DAL COPPER POLY..
X	90	DQE-21463-DAL DUREX GOLD POLY.
A	01	DQE-9000-DAL BLACK. (NO SWATCH)

SPECIFY { DAL– For DITZ-LAC® Automotive Lacquer
{ DQE– For DITZCO® Quickset Enamel

DITZLER COLOR DIVISION
PITTSBURGH PLATE GLASS COMPANY
Detroit 4, Michigan
Form 5811

(Recreated for this publication for space and readability.)

1958 Edsel interior colors

* also exterior body color

EDSEL

	Color
2714-H	Sunset Coral*
2715-H	Spruce Green Metallic*
2716	Ice Green*
2717	Royal Blue Metallic*
2720	Powder Blue*
2721-H	Ember Red*
2722	Chalk Pink*
2723	Gold Metallic*
2724	Silver Gray Metallic*
2725	Turquoise*
2726	Jonquil Yellow*
2727-H	Copper Metallic*
83074	Dark Brown Metallic

83074 Dark Brown Metallic

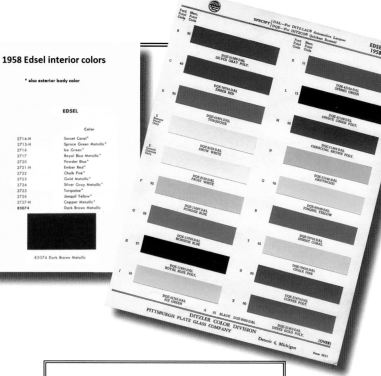

1958 Edsel Interior Colors

	Color
2714-H	Sunset Coral*
2715-H	Spruce Green Metallic*
2716	Ice Green*
2717	Royal Blue Metallic*
2720	Powder Blue*
2721-H	Ember Red*
2722	Chalk Pink*
2723	Gold Metallic*
2724	Silver Gray Metallic*
2725	Turquoise*
2726	Jonquil Yellow*
2727-H	Cooper Metallic*
83074	Dark Brown Metallic

*also exterior body color

83074 Dark Brown Metallic

Opposite Page: A four-door Edsel Citation at a museum in Michigan.

Fast Facts

Did you know?

- The Edsel's vertical front grille was inspired by the 1937 LaSalle, which left a lasting impression on Chief Designer Roy Brown, who worked for GM as a designer early in his career.
- But don't be too harsh on him. Just before starting work on the Edsel, Brown designed the 1955 Lincoln "Futura" show car, which went on to become the "Batmobile" in the 1966 hit television series, "*Batman*."
- Market research that served as the basis for the Edsel's existence was gathered five years before the car was launched when the U.S. economy was healthy. It didn't account for the first and most severe economic recession since the end of World War II, in 1957, and the worst post-war automotive market. That, more so than the grille design, doomed the Edsel from the start.
- The car initially was referred to as the "E" car (for Experimental) during its development and pre-launch "teaser" campaign.
- The name "Edsel" was selected by Special Products Division General Manager Richard Krafve, after reviewing nearly 8,000 suggestions from Ford's advertising firm, Ford employees, and renowned poet laureate Marianne Moore.
- Many innovative firsts that were introduced on the 1958 Edsel still are being used today, according to *edsel.com*. They include:
  - Transmissions that lock in park until the ignition key is turned.
  - Slant-forward seats to provide better shoulder support.
  - Triple thermostat cooling system during warm-ups for increased fuel economy and heater performance.
  - Front-mounted oil filter dipstick for easy access.
  - Electronic hood release from inside the car.
- If you think the Edsel's horse shoe grille was the kiss of death, check out the grille on the 2019 Bugatti Divo. Sure, it looks like a space ship. It costs $5.8 million, and top speed is "limited" to 236 mph. But there's no mistaking the shape of the front grille.
- The last Edsel in 1960 had no horse collar grille, and it looked pretty much like every other large American car of that era. But by then it was too late to save the Edsel from its fate and place in history.
- Today, fewer than 6,000 Edsels are estimated to have survived.

Opposite page: This front-facing photo shows just how radically the '57 Chevy's grille changed from the 1955 model in the ad (page 22), courtesy of *oldcaradvertising.com*

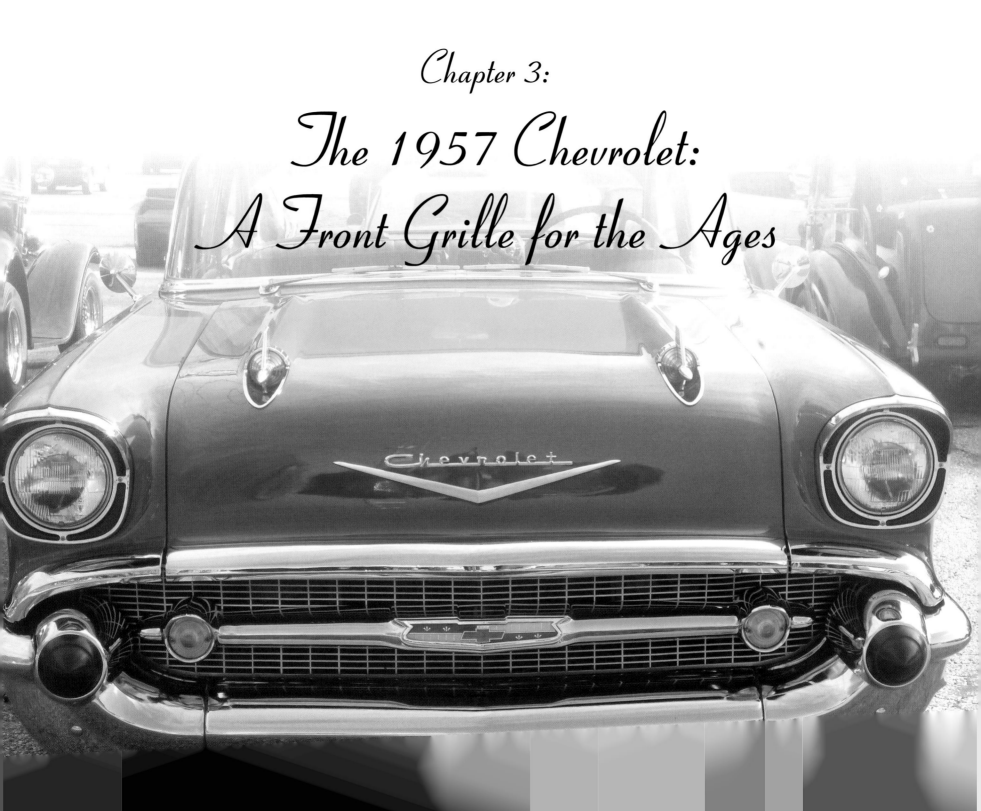

Chapter 3:

The 1957 Chevrolet:
A Front Grille for the Ages

Perhaps no car better defines the 1950s and the rock 'n roll era than the 1957 Chevy, with its signature wide-oval lower bonnet front grille, "Dagmar" bumper guards and subtle (by the standards of the times) tail fins. In all its various body styles – including the '57 Bel Air convertible and Nomad station wagon, which many experts consider the prettiest long tops to ever come out of Detroit – the '57 Chevy is as iconic as they come. It remains one of the most appealing automotive designs ever, and among the most desirable classics to own.

One of the big reasons behind the '57 Chevy's timeless appeal is the front grille, which was designed on the fly as a response to the public's luke-warm response to the 1955 Chevy's Ferrari-inspired grille, and the introduction of Ford's totally new 1957 body styles. There was nothing plain-Jane about the '57 Chevy's front grille, including two prominent but definitely not Cadillac-sized "Dagmar" bumper guards and optional black rubber "pasties" in each corner of the grille. (For more on Dagmar bumpers, see Chapter 4.)

The story behind the development of the '57 Chevy and its front grille is as classic as the car itself. According to classic car blogger Bruce Troxell, Chevrolet's initial plan for 1957 was to introduce a totally new car to build on the success of the 1955 and 1956 models. Delays in the new model's development forced Chevy management to reconsider their decision at the last minute and go to plan 'B' – a full face-lift of the 1956 Chevrolet. Designers kept the rear deck lid, the roof, and the doors from the '56 and proceeded to fulfill legendary designer Harley Earl's desire for the '57 to look "as big as possible."

Clare MacKichan, who oversaw the design, remembered the whole team was under great pressure to differentiate the '57 Chevy from the previous model. And when it was all done, most of the designers who worked on the crash development program didn't like its looks. Many were concerned the car wouldn't sell.

Yet when the 1957 Chevrolet Bel Air was unveiled on Dec. 8, 1956, it was an instant hit and the designers had succeeded beyond their wildest dreams. Promoted as a "daring new departure in design for 1957," Chevrolet built more than 1.5 million units, in 19 body styles and 460 model/color combinations, according to *Hemmings Motor News*. More than 700,000 two-door 1957 Bel Airs alone were sold. And the Bel Air was only the second-best selling model in the Chevrolet lineup. The top sales honor went to the mid-line 210 four-door sedan.

The grille represented a radical departure from the blander 1955 and '56 models. Chevrolet's engineer manuals heralded the new look in grand terms.

"Reproportioned and redesigned to extend across the entire width of the front end of the car, the components all contribute to the prominent impression of vehicle width, length and a lower overall height.

"Styled into one unit, the grille-bumper combination consists of three main elements blending into sheet metal contours. The upper bar extended along the lower hood edge, then arches down to the heavy lower element which is the bumper proper. A lattice pattern aluminum grille screen, featuring long rectangles, form the background for the control grille bar, containing the parking lights at either end and the Chevrolet medallion in the center."

Twin hood ornaments replaced the single jet ornament that were so common on GM models in previous years, offering a sharp accent to the new front treatment.

Opposite page: The iconic 1957 Chevrolet Bel Air is the definitive '50s classic. Its distinctive front grille features two "Dagmar" bumper guards and optional black rubber "pasties." This Bel Air is owned by Paul Caiola in Monroe, CT.

Chevrolet's advertising promoted the car's daring design departure and prominently featured the car's signature front grille. Like most of GM's cars from that time, the '57 Chevy was inspired by jet fighters. "Chevrolet wanted its customers to know they were sitting behind something almost supersonic," according to *Hemmings Motor News*. The public agreed. Ads courtesy of *oldcaradvertising.com*.

Today, the two-door hardtop Bel Airs, Nomads and convertibles are considered the most collectible, but with the supply of unrestored candidates dwindling, interest in the two-door post sedans and four-door sedans is on the rise.

"Just 6,264 Nomads were built, and they are highly prized," according to *Hemmings*.

An interesting side note on the 57 Chevy is this little-known fact: The interior design was heavily influenced by GM's "Damsels of Design," a team of female designers that Earl hired to add a woman's point of view to automobile styling.

According to David Temple, the author of *Chevrolet's of the 1950's: A Decade of Technological Innovation*, this team left its mark on the '57. Multi-colored fabric inserts and pleated vinyl upholstery that were featured in a Bel Air convertible prototype became popular additions throughout the lineup.

Grille Tech Sheet: 1957 Chevrolet

Manufacturer: Chevrolet Motor Division, General Motors, Detroit, MI.
Body By: Fisher Body Division General Motors (Detroit)
Body Styles: 2-and 4-door post sedan (pillars between windows and full frame) 2-and 4-door pillar less hardtop, 2-door convertible, 2-door Handyman Wagon, 4-door Townsman Wagon, 2-door Utility Sedan, 2-door Nomad Sport Wagon.
Trim Levels: 150 (basic), 210 (upgrade) and Bel Air (deluxe)

Production Numbers (by Trim Level)
- 150: 146,080
- 210: 651,358
- Bel Air: 702,040

1957 model year production: 1,499,748

Engines – Standard options

1. 235-cubic inch L block 6-cylinder ("Blue Flame Six")1bbl carb 140 HP/210 ft. lbs. Torque
2. 265-cubic inch V block 8-cylinder ("Turbo Fire V-8") 2bbl carb 162 HP/257 ft. lbs. Torque
3. 283-cubic inch V block 8-cylinder ("Turbo Fire V-8") 2bbl carb 185 HP/ 275 ft. lbs. Torque
4. 283-cubic inch V block 8-cylinder ("Super Turbo Fire V-8")4bbl carb 220 HP/300 ft. lbs. Torque

Optional Engines

1. 283-cubic inch V Block 8-Cylinder ("Taskmaster V-8")

1957 Chevrolet Colors

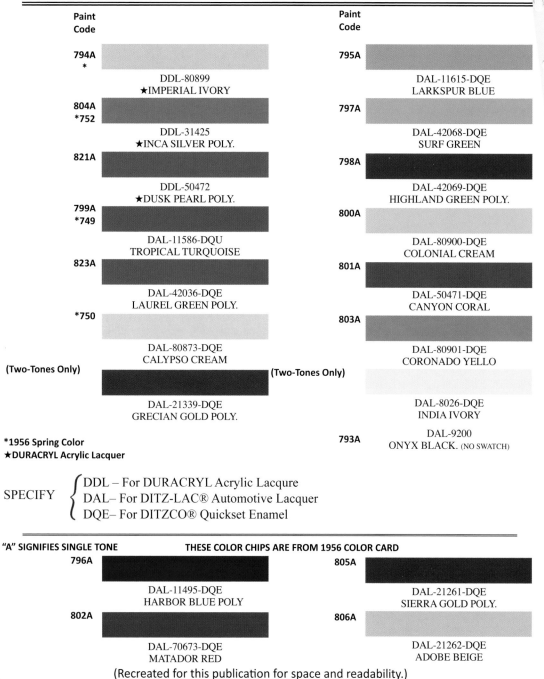

Paint Code		Paint Code	
794A *	DDL-80899 ★IMPERIAL IVORY	795A	DAL-11615-DQE LARKSPUR BLUE
804A *752	DDL-31425 ★INCA SILVER POLY.	797A	DAL-42068-DQE SURF GREEN
821A	DDL-50472 ★DUSK PEARL POLY.	798A	DAL-42069-DQE HIGHLAND GREEN POLY.
799A *749	DAL-11586-DQU TROPICAL TURQUOISE	800A	DAL-80900-DQE COLONIAL CREAM
823A	DAL-42036-DQE LAUREL GREEN POLY.	801A	DAL-50471-DQE CANYON CORAL
*750	DAL-80873-DQE CALYPSO CREAM	803A	DAL-80901-DQE CORONADO YELLO
(Two-Tones Only)	DAL-21339-DQE GRECIAN GOLD POLY.	(Two-Tones Only)	DAL-8026-DQE INDIA IVORY
		793A	DAL-9200 ONYX BLACK. (NO SWATCH)

*1956 Spring Color
★DURACRYL Acrylic Lacquer

SPECIFY {
DDL – For DURACRYL Acrylic Lacqure
DAL– For DITZ-LAC® Automotive Lacquer
DQE– For DITZCO® Quickset Enamel
}

"A" SIGNIFIES SINGLE TONE   THESE COLOR CHIPS ARE FROM 1956 COLOR CARD

796A	DAL-11495-DQE HARBOR BLUE POLY	805A	DAL-21261-DQE SIERRA GOLD POLY.
802A	DAL-70673-DQE MATADOR RED	806A	DAL-21262-DQE ADOBE BEIGE

(Recreated for this publication for space and readability.)

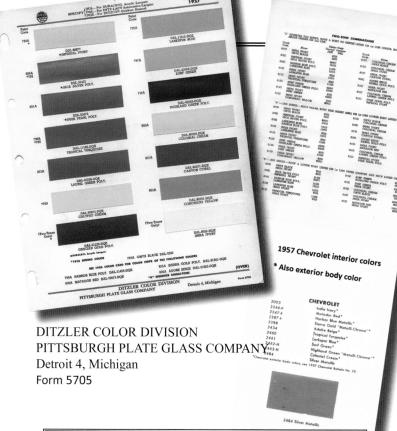

DITZLER COLOR DIVISION
PITTSBURGH PLATE GLASS COMPANY
Detroit 4, Michigan
Form 5705

1957 Chevrolet interior colors
* Also exterior body color

2484 Silver Metallic

1957 Chevrolet Interior Colors

	Color
2003	India Ivory*
2246-H	Matador Red*
2247-H	Harbor Blue Metallic*
2287-H	Sierra Gold "Metalli-Chrome"*
2288	Adobe Beige*
2434	Tropical Turquoise*
2460	Lakespur Blue*
2461	Surf Green*
2462-H	Highland Green "Metalli-Chrome"*
2463-H	Colonial Cream*
2484	Silver Metallic

*Chevrolet exterior body colors, see 1957 Chevrolet Bulletin No. 29.

2484 Silver Metallic

Current Values by condition from Hagerty

Highest and lowest production type from each Series

SERIES 150

- 2-door post sedan (70,774)
  #1 $42,700 / #2 $31,100 / #3 $20,400 / #4$ 14,400
- 2-door utility sedan (8,300)
  #1 $31,900 / #2 $22,300 / #3 $13,100 / #4 $9700.00

SERIES 210

- 4-door post sedan (260,401)
  #1 $29,600 / #2 $18,900 / #3 13,600 / #4 $9,500

- 4-door sport sedan (Hardtop) (16,178)
  #1 $36,600 / #2 $28,300 / #3 $21,700 / #4$16,100

BEL AIR

- 4-door post sedan (254,331)
  #1 $29,900 / #2 $23,100 / #3 $17,700 / #4 $13,200

- 2-Door Nomad Wagon (6,103)
  #1 $102,000 / #2 $72,400 / #3 $61,100 / #4 $35,100

Production Colors: The Color Palette for 1957 was just like the numbers and models produced – extensive. Several color charts exist. Many colors were either special order only or used on specially "one off" cars built for GM executives and benefactors of the corporation. The palette featured 31 possibilities!

The evolution of Chevrolet's front grille between 1955 and 1957 is evident in this photo of four Bel Air's parked together at a Tri-Five Chevy show. The basic, European-inspired rectangular shaped grille on the '55 (second from left) became wider and extended across the entire width of the car in 1956 (second from right). In 1957, Chevy's design stylists took the gloves off to counter the dramatic lines of Chrysler's Forward Look with an oval shaped chrome grille that framed two Dagmar nose cones. The designers didn't think it would sell, but the public disagreed.

Two-Tone Combinations

"C" SIGNIFIES 2100 SERIES. ROOF & BODY TO CENTER LISTED ON 1ST LINE; CENTER, HOOD, REAR DECK & BODY ABOVE FENDER ON 2ND LINE.

Comb. Code	Name	Ditzler Code Enamel DQE	Ditzler Code Lacquer DAL
807C	India Ivory Onyx Black	8026 9200	
808C	Imperial Ivory Inca Silver Poly.	80877 31425	
809C	Harbor Blue Poly. Larkspur Blue	11495 11615	
810C	India Ivory Larkspur Blue	8026 11615	
811C	India Ivory Tropical Turquoise	8026 11586	
812C	Surf Green Highland Green Poly.	42068 42069	
813C	India Ivory Surf Green	8026 42068	
814C	India Ivory Coronado Yellow	8026 80901	
815C	Colonial Cream Onyx Black	80900 9200	
816C	Colonial Cream India Ivory	80900 8026	
817D	India Ivory Canyon Coral	8026 50471	
818C	Adobe Beige Sierra Gold Poly.	21262 21261	
819C	India Ivory Matador Red	8026 70673	
820C	Colonial Cream Laurel Green Poly.	80900 42036	
822C	Dusk Pearl Poly. Imperial Ivory	50472 80877	

"D" SIGNIFIES 2400 SERIES. ROOF PILLAR, BODY SIDE INSERT AREA ON 1ST LIN; LOWER BODY LISTED ON 2ND LINE.

Comb. Code	Name	Ditzler Code Enamel DQE	Ditzler Code Lacquer DAL
807D	India Ivory Onyx Black	8026 9200	
808D	Imperial Ivory Inca Silver Poly.	80877 31425	
809D	Larkspur Blue Harbor Blue Poly.	11615 11495	
810D	India Ivory Larkspur Blue	8026 11615	
811D	India Ivory Tropical Turquoise	8026 11586	
812D	Surf Green Highland Green Poly.	42068 42069	
813D	India Ivory Surf Green	8026 42068	
814D	India Ivory Coronado Yellow	8026 80901	
815D	Onyx Black Colonial Cream	9200 80900	
816D	India Ivory Colonial Cream	8026 80900	
817D	India Ivory Canyon Coral	8026 50471	
818D	Adobe Beige Sierra Gold Poly.	21262 21261	
819D	India Ivory Matador Red	8026 70673	
820D	Colonial Cream Laurel Green Poly.	80900 42036	
822D	Dusk Pearl Poly. Imperial Ivory	50472 80877	

"E" SIGNIFIES 1500 SERIES. ROOF & LOWER BODY LISTED ON 1ST LINE; UPPER QUARTER & DECK LISTED ON 2ND LINE.

Comb. Code	Name	Ditzler Code Enamel DQE	Ditzler Code Lacquer DAL
807E	Onyx Black India Ivory	9200 8026	
808E	Inca Silver Poly. Imperial Ivory	31425 80877	
809E	Harbor Blue Poly. Larkspur Blue	11495 11615	
810E	Larkspur Blue India Ivory	11615 8026	
811E	Tropical Turquoise India Ivory	11586 8026	
812E	Surf Green Highland Green Poly.	42068 42069	
813E	Surf Green India Ivory	42068 8026	
815E	Colonial Cream Onyx Black	80900 9200	
816E	Colonial Cream India Ivory	80900 8026	
819E	Matador Red India Ivory	70673 8026	

It's hard to believe now, but consumers were initially reluctant to buy the 1957 Chevy because it was the first car to offer tubeless tires, a technology that some just didn't trust. This '57 Bel Air, complete with rubber pasties, is owned by Ralph Renzulli in Monroe, CT.

The beautifully new Bel Air Sport Sedan—one of 20 new Chevies. Sweet and low—and longer for '57!

'57 CHEVROLET! SWEET, SMOOTH AND SASSY!

Chevy goes 'em all one better for '57 with a daring new departure in design (looks longer and lower, and it is!), exclusive new Triple-Turbine Turboglide automatic drive, a new V8 and a bumper crop of new ideas including fuel injection!

Chevy's new beauty wins going away! Body by Fisher, of course.

Chevy's new and Chevy shows it—from its daring new grille and stylish, lower bonnet to the saucy new slant of its High-Fashion rear fenders. It's longer, too, and looks it.

And new style is just the start. There's new velvety V8 power that ranges up to 245* h.p. Then, you've a choice of *two* automatic drives as extra-cost options. There's an even finer Powerglide, and new Turboglide with Triple-Turbine take-off.

Go see the new car that goes 'em all one better. Your Chevrolet dealer's got it! . . . Chevrolet Division of General Motors, Detroit 2, Michigan.

1 USA
'57 CHEVROLET

*A special 270-h.p. engine also available at extra cost. Also revolutionary Ramjet fuel injection engines with up to 283 h.p. in Corvette and passenger car models.

28

Fast Facts

Did you know?

- Before Chevrolet's major facelift in 1957, many new car buyers were turning to restyled Fords. That attitude spilled over into 1957. Despite the introduction of the newly designed model – rival Ford outsold Chevrolet by 170,000 cars for the first time since 1935, according to *howstuffworks.com*.
- The main cause of the sales shift to Ford was that the '57 Chevrolet was the first car to offer tubeless tires, and many consumers initially did not trust the new tubeless design. Also, Ford's introduction of an all-new body styling (to counter Chrysler's Forward Look) that was longer, lower and wider than the previous year's offerings helped Ford sales, according to *1957Ford.com*.
- Though it is recognized as *THE* iconic American car, few considered the '57 Chevy anything special. Classic car historians have even called it the Toyota Camry of its time.
- Nevertheless, Chevrolet produced 1.5 million cars in 1957. Only 47,652 of those were convertibles. And of those convertibles, only 68 were ordered with fuel-injection. These cars were called "fuelies."
- Despite the '57's cosmetic makeover, it was essentially the same body that Chevrolet used in 1955 and 1956. As noted in Chapter 3, Chevrolet spiced things up a bit with the addition of fins and the totally redesigned front grille.
- The front mesh grille had a horizontal bar featuring a Chevy emblem in the center and round parking lights at each end. Dual hood ornaments set off the hood.
- The 1957 Chevy also won 26 NASCAR "convertible races," which was more wins than any other make*. The dominance of the 1957 Chevrolet prompted NASCAR's ban on fuel-injected cars. In April of 1957, NASCAR rewrote the rules to establish a four-barrel carburetor-only rule. The fuel-injection ban lasted until the Generation-Six cars of 2012.
- The 1957 Chevy Bel Air, with a 283 cubic inch engine, went from a standing start to 60 miles per hour in 9.9 seconds and cleared the quarter mile in 17.5 seconds. While slow by today's super-charged standards, these times were exceptional in 1957, when bias tires, slushy transmissions and overly soft suspensions were the norm.
- 1957 was the third and final year of the high roofline, short wheelbase, "shoebox" Chevys. A much larger and heavier X-frame model debuted in 1958.

*http://www.classic-car-history.com/

Chapter 4:
Dagmar Bumpers: Do You Get the Point?

Popular American television personality Dagmar was not the inspiration for what eventually become known as "Dagmar Bumpers" on Cadillacs and many other popular GM models in the 1950s. But the public didn't care, and by 1954 they just called them (and bought them) in pairs as they saw them. The point was well taken by automotive designers throughout Detroit. Cadillac illustration courtesy of *caddyinfo.com*.

"Dagmar (D-HAG-MAR) Bumpers" is a slang term for the chrome conical-shaped styling elements that began to appear on the front bumper/grille assemblies of certain American automobiles as the U.S. entered World War II. They reached their peak in both size and popularity in the mid-1950s, but smaller versions continued to appear on popular models into the early 1960s.

The term is derived from the notable physical attributes of Dagmar,[1] a buxom early 1950s television personality known for wearing low-cut gowns and pronounced conical bra cups. She was amused by the tribute. If you're younger than 60, you probably don't remember, but Dagmar – born Virginia Ruth Egnor – was once described by *Life* magazine as a "national institution." A nationwide poll of editors in the 1950s voted Dagmar "the most photogenic girl on TV." Egnor's Dagmar was the stereotypical dumb blonde comic relief on the NBC program, *Broadway Open House*, which aired in 1950 and 1951.

As American automakers' use of chrome grew more flamboyant, the Dagmars grew more prominent. Black rubber tips known as pasties[2] were even added onto the 1957 Cadillac Eldorado Brougham and other GM models as optional safety features.

Above: This stunning 1957 Cadillac Seville in Bahama Blue Metallic (one of several blue exterior colors on Cadillac's paint pallet that year) is owned by Peter Büttner in Lauda Gerlachsheim, Germany. The Dagmar bumper guards and protective rubber pasties had become standard issue on all Cadillacs models by 1957, and eventually disappeared in 1959.

Although nosecone bumper protectors were quite common features on many American font grilles by the mid-1950s, Cadillac was the undisputed king of Dagmars. The nosecones on the 1957 Cadillac Series 62 convertible (left) were massive and set high atop the front grille just below the hood line. Owned by Frank Fernicola in East Haven, CT.

1. https://en.wikipedia.org/wiki/Dagmar_(American_actress)
2. https://en.wikipedia.org/wiki/Pasties

Though Dagmars are most often associated with the grilles of the 1950s, they originally appeared in a subtle form on the 1942 Cadillac as bumper over-riders. The inspirational linkage to fighter aircraft of the day is apparent in this 1942 Cadillac ad, courtesy of the Automotive History Preservation Society.

But regardless of the name, the conical-shaped bumper guards were conceived by Harley Earl, GM's legendary vice president of design, to mimic artillery shells.[2] Placed inboard of the headlights on front bumpers of Cadillacs, they were intended to convey the image of speeding projectiles while protecting the vehicles' front ends in collisions.

A 2006 *Hemmings Motor News* report claims Earl never set out to up the "car as sex object" ante by flanking the grille assembly of the 1953 Cadillac with nosecones that would be perceived as something quite different. That's just the way it happened. It was the height of the Cold War, the zenith of the Jet Age. Military, aeronautical and space-age motifs were everywhere, from the refrigerator, to the television, to the mixer your mom used to whip up batches of cookies.

While the bumper extensions on the 1953 Cadillac would inextricably be linked with sex, they were an evolution of a design that had been evolving since World War II.

The last M-24 tank rolled off the Cadillac production line in August of 1945, and work on the 1946 Cadillac was in full swing by the first week in October. Like everyone else's car, the 1946 Cadillac was a hastily thrown-together version of the 1942 Series Sixty-Two.

In 1942, Cadillac featured a wide, egg-crate grille with round parking lamps in the upper corners. Centering the massive front bumper were a pair of "bumper over-riders" with missile-like projections. It was a simple styling exercise, something that added a bit more authority to the Cadillac's already imposing grille-work.

By the mid-'50s Cadillac's bumper protectors had grown to enormous proportions, as seen here in this automotive graphic illustration of a 1954 Cadillac owned by Gary DellaVecchio in Oxford, CT. Art by Automotive Artist JoepeP (opposite page). The real-life Cadillac, and it's brilliantly chromed Dagmars, is seen here at a car show in Stratford, Conn.

By 1954, Dagmars were front and center on all of Buick's models and advertising. But some things were better left unsaid. Buick's 1954 dealer brochure described the new Roadmaster's grille like this: "The swift, sleek lines of the Convertible model emphasize the breathtaking beauty of the new ROADMASTER. Note the tasteful sweep of the fender spear, the new four port moldings, the gleaming distinction of the grille ..." Dealer brochures courtesy of Automotive History Preservation Society.

Below: A 1954 Buick Skylark Convertible as it appeared in a dealer brochure.

1954 BUICK

When better automobiles are built BUICK will build them

the beautiful buy

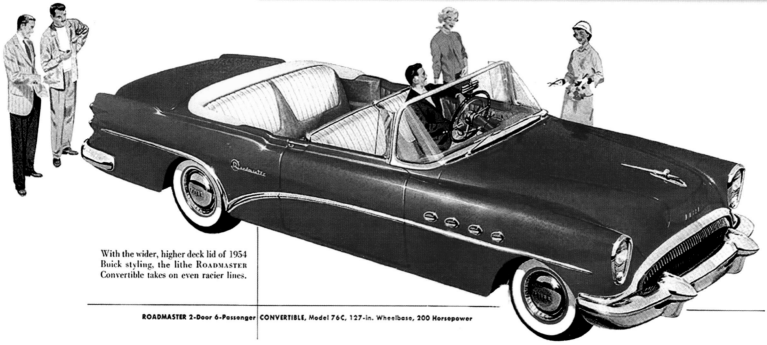

With the wider, higher deck lid of 1954 Buick styling, the lithe ROADMASTER Convertible takes on even racier lines.

ROADMASTER 2-Door 6-Passenger CONVERTIBLE, Model 76C, 127-in. Wheelbase, 200 Horsepower

Darwin's Theory of Evolution states that beneficial mutations within the genetic code that aid an organism's survival will be passed down from generation to generation. And so it was at Cadillac. Post-war Cadillacs began sporting true conical bumper guards in 1946, as soon as commercial production resumed following World War II. Since the 1946 Cadillac sold with bumper extensions, and the 1948 Cadillac sold with even larger extensions, they grew in size and stature over the ensuing years. On 1951 models, some were even raised into the grille.

In 1950, the bumper extensions became larger, and the grille was flanked by a pair of fog lamps. Depending on the model, the space was occupied by a pair of softball-sized chrome fillers. This design theme would stay constant until 1953.

In 1953, the bumper guards became bolder, and stylistically significant. Earl's idea, as executed by Cadillac designer Ed Glowacke, was that the bumper guards would mimic exaggerated artillery shells, to symbolize speed and power. Each successive year, the bumper guards became more and more massive. In 1957, all-new safety enhancing black rubber pasties made an already prominent design element even more obvious. They continued to become more pronounced in size through 1958, but ironically enough were eliminated in the 1959 Cadillac redesign to draw attention to the car's outrageously large fins.

In 1958, Cadillac stylists sized down the nosecones (slightly) and re-positioned them on the outer edges of the grille just below the newly introduced quad headlights. This '58 is owned by Frank Fernicola in East Haven, CT.

"88" 4-DOOR SEDAN

By the mid-'50s, Cadillac was not the only brand to sport Dagmars. Buick and Oldsmobile offered more subdued "snub-nose" offerings in 1954, as did Ford. Above: a 1954 Oldsmobile from a dealer brochure, courtesy Automotive History Preservation Society. Below right: a 1952 Mercury Monterey, owned by Norm Mercier of Monroe, CT.

Buick added Dagmars on its 1954 and 1955 models; in '54, they were part of the bumper assembly, and then they were moved into the grille in '55. More subdued, snub-nose bullets appeared on Oldsmobiles, Pontiacs and some Chevy models, most notably the iconic '57 Chevy.

GM was not alone in its fascination with Dagmars. Mercury sported Dagmars from 1953 through the 1956 model year. Lincoln wanted in on the action and added Dagmars to its model lineup in 1960, with a black rubber ring separating the body from the chrome tip.

Full-sized Chevys in 1961 and 1963 also had small rubber Dagmars on the front bumper, and the 1962 Ford Galaxie also offered small rubber Dagmars as options.

By the late '50s, American car designers began to shed both rear tailfins and bumper guards. And by 1961, the party was over. America had decided that there really was such a thing as too much of a good thing and turned away from such styling excess in droves. Cars of the later 1960s were minimalist and austere compared to those from the immediate post-war period.

Cars as late as the 1961 Impala still had small Dagmars with rubber pasties. This stunning white and red convertible is owned by Paul Mclaughlin of Trumbull, CT.

Fast Facts

Did you know?

- Dagmar, the statuesque, busty blonde who became one of television's first major female stars, did not work for or have an association with any major American automobile company in the 1950s.
- Her real name was Virginia Ruth Egnor.
- Dagmar was a virtual unknown who became a sensation after she was given a sidekick job on Jerry Lester's 1950 TV show, as well as the new name. She soon became a bigger star than Lester, who eventually quit. Dagmar then went on to become a big celebrity in the '50s.
- She appeared regularly on Milton Berle's *Texaco Star Theater*, the *Bob Hope Show* and the *Colgate Comedy Hour*.
- Dagmar had one hit record with Frank Sinatra, "*Mama Will Bark*," that was produced by Mitch Miller at Columbia Records. Sinatra hated it and refused to work with Miller.
- Though Dagmar bumpers appeared on many American front ends over the course of three decades, there is little doubt that the biggest and most exaggerated Dagmar bumpers appeared on Cadillacs of the mid-'50s.
- Dagmars made a comeback on a much smaller scale when British automaker Triumph added an oversized pair of protruding rubber bumper blocks to the lower grille lip of its 1974 lineup to meet U.S. safety regulations. The automotive press named them "Sabrinas" after the statuesque British actress who mimicked Dagmar's look.

This two-door Sportsman Hardtop is owned by Phil Convertito of Stratford, CT.

Chapter 5:
1957 DeSoto Fireflite:
A Forward-Looking
Grille That Brings Up the Rear

The 1957 DeSoto Fireflite sports one of Detroit's all-time classic grilles, courtesy of Virgil Exner's revolutionary "Forward Look" design. But unlike many of the other featured cars in this book, the Fireflite's front grille is overshadowed by its larger-than-life Jetson-era stacked rear triple headlights.

Even today, a glimpse of the car's rear quickly brings to mind the classic Terri Hatcher line from Seinfeld: "They're real and they're spectacular!"

That's exactly what Exner wanted for the entire Chrysler lineup in 1957 – a bold, signature feature that would command immediate attention and leave the rest of the domestic auto industry with models that looked like yesterday's news. Exner succeeded largely because the Forward Look captured the public's attention and forced GM and Ford to quickly develop new looks for their outdated automobiles.

It should be noted that Exner was no stranger to innovative front grille designs. At GM, he patented the combination "bumper grille" used on the 1942 Buick. While at Studebaker, he developed the "split grille" on 1941 models that foreshadowed what was yet to come from Pontiac. His makeover of Chrysler's 1950 models also had a highly stylized grille feature.

Exner's front-end designs typically featured long, leading fenders with low hood lines that plunged between the fenders to meet with a shallow, horizontal grille. This was his interpretation of post-war Italian coachwork styling, and its influence is easy to spot across the entire Chrysler lineup.

Of course, there was much more to the Fireflite's Forward Look in 1957 than just the tail lights. The Fireflite featured radically new body styling – all of the '57 DeSoto bodies were lower and longer than the '56 models, and they had significantly lower profiles than the upside-down bathtubs at GM and Ford. Chassis engineering had been enhanced, as well, for a smoother ride. Veteran automotive tester Tom McCahill declared the Fireflite's unique torsion-bar front suspension "so far superior to anything else being made in this country that the contest isn't even close." This innovative suspension gave the Fireflite superb handing in tight curves and corners, powered by a mighty 341-cubic inch Hemi V8.

Had it not been for the soaring rear tail lights, the Fireflite's wide-mouth grille would surely be considered the most prominent feature on the car. When judged on its own merits the Fireflite's front end treatment is eye-catching in a very different way. While the rear tail lights made it look like the car was about to launch into space, the front end gave the Fireflite an appealing personality.

The striking appearance started with the positioning of the twin headlights –separate and above the grille with cut-back notches on the sides of the hood – making it appear as if the car has eyes that are looking directly at you. Add in the chrome grille, which wraps around the entire lower front end of the car, and the Fireflite seems to be smiling. Not a huge grin, mind you, but a friendly look that gave the car an inviting warmth that balanced the hard-to-miss rear end.

Is it any wonder that DeSoto ads of the day promoted the Fireflite as both "Delovely and Dynamic?"

Not everything on the grille was radically new. Two bullet type bumperettes – mini-Dagmars in honor of the most prominent physical features of the television personality who went by that name – grace the middle of the bumper's lower lip. These were quite common throughout the '50s, (see Chapter 4) and serve as a pointed reminder that the Forward Look wasn't above capitalizing on the obvious.

The Fireflite also had a "V" shape at the end of the front fenders intersecting the top chrome molding, and a chrome ornament on the top of the fender at the front. These were accentuated by individual cutouts for the single lamp headlights and no chrome lip on the hood. The headlights became duals later in the model run.

Opposite page: The rear tail lights and front grille were the featured attractions in this composite of publicity photos from DeSoto in 1957. The quad headlights in the lower corner were added later in the model year.

1957 Desoto Colors

FIREDOME CODE S-25 AND FIREFLITE CODE 2-26

Paint Code		Paint Code		Paint Code	
BBB *	DQE-11577-DAL CAPRI BLUE	GGG	DQE-31321-DAL CHARCOAL GRAY POLY.	LLL	DQE-8036-DAL WHTE
CCC	DQE-11522-DAL AZURE BLUE POLY.	HHH	DQE-70691-DAL FIESTA RED	RRR	DQE-60234-DAL MANDARIN RUST
DDD	DQE-42024-DAL SEAFOAM GREEN	JJJ	DQE-50445-DAL MUSCATEL MAROON POLY.	XXX	DQE-21279-DAL SAHARA TAN
EEE	DQE-41954-DAL TAMARACK GREEN POLY.	KKK	DQE-80905-DAL SUNSET YELLOW	ZZZ	DQE-21282-DAL SPICE BROWN POLY.
FFF	DQE-31347-DAL DOVE GRAY	AAA	DQE-9000-DAL BLACK (NO SWATCH)	1956 (Two-Tones Only)	DQE-21293-DAL ADVENTURER GOLD POLY.

FIRESWEEP CODE S-27

BBB *	DQE-11531-DAL LAGOON BLUE	AAA	DQE-9000-DAL BLACK (NO SWATCH)	MMM	DQE-8121-DAL FROSTY WHITE
CCC	DQE-11529-DAL SEATONE BLUE POLY.	FFF	DQE-31410-DAL DAWN GRAY	NNN	DQE-11522-DAL LIGHT AQUA
DDD	DQE-41960-DAL MIST GREEN	GGG	DQE-31410-DAL DAWN GRAY	SSS	DQE-70698-DAL DUSTY ORANGE
EEE	DQE-41496-DAL LEAF GREEN POLY	KKK	DQE-80850-DAL SUNBURST YELLOW		DQE-41961-DAL SAMOA GREEN

SEE COLOR CHIPS SHOWN FOR MODELS S-25, S-26 ON THE FOLLOWING COLORS.

HHH -DQE-70691-DAL
FIESTA RED

JJJ -DQE-50445-DAL
MUSCATEL MAROON POLY.

DITZLER COLOR DIVISION
PITTSBURGH PLATE GLASS COMPANY
Detroit 4, Michigan
Form 55703

SPECIFY { DAL– For DITZ-LAC® Automotive Lacquer
{ DQE– For DITZCO® Quickset Enamel

(Recreated for this publication for space and readability.)

Note:
Specify model number S-25, S-26 or S-27 when using paint code letters. Color combinations can be identified by the arrangement of the paint code letters.
For Example:

Singe Tone
AAA, DDD, Etc.
"AAA" = Black, 9000
"DDD" = Seaform Green 42024

Standard Two-Tones
ADD
"A"= Upper, Black 900
"DD" = Lower, Seafoam Green

Two-Tones with Sweep
First Letter "A" = Upper, Black 9000
Second Letter "D" = Lower, Seafoam Green 42024
Third Letter "A" = Sweep, Black 900

According to the Automotive History Preservation Society, the top-of-the-line Fireflite S26 featured a 341-inch eight cylinder HEMI engine, and plenty of bells and whistles including:

- "Fireflite" rear fender nameplates, and front fender side molding medallions.
- Dual-color sweep moldings were standard trim on hardtops and convertibles. The standard side trim used on sedans and station wagons consisted of the upper molding sections only.
- The convertible coupe used a distinctive, dome-like windshield, which would become standard for all Sportsman models for 1958. Front fender top chrome ornaments were used on some Fireflite models. The six-passenger station wagon was referred to as the "Shopper," while the nine-passenger version was called the "Explorer." Torqueflite automatic transmission, foam seat cushions, backup lights, and wheel covers were all standard.

Many auto enthusiasts consider 1957 the high-water mark for DeSoto, and the Fireflite Sportsman 2-Door Hardtop to be one of the all-time greatest designs to emerge from Detroit. Yet for all its head-turning looks and power, at the time the DeSoto brand was on a fast track to extinction. According to *Old Cars Weekly*, DeSoto ranked 11th among U.S. automakers in 1957 with 117,474 cars built. But that figured plunged sharply in 1958, as the U.S. economy suffered its first major downturn since the end of World War II.

"The Fireflite model lasted only through 1960, when it was relegated to bottom-tier status as only the Fireflite and Adventurer lineups remained," the journal reports. "In November of 1960, Chrysler pulled the plug altogether on the DeSoto brand, leaving only a handful of 1961 models for dealers to try to unload."

It is a pity because for a brief period the Fireflite truly was a delovely and dynamic example of how Detroit designs could captivate the public both coming and going.

FIREFLITE 4-DOOR *Sportsman*

The Fireflite four-door sedan was the biggest seller in DeSoto's 1957 lineup, with 11,565 units rolling off the assembly line. The sweeping front grilled, topped off by the stacked Jetson-era rear tail lights, ensure that it would never be considered a "plain Jane" sedan.

1957 DeSoto Interior Colors

DQE-8036-DAL **WHITE**	DQE-8036-DAL **WHITE**
DQE-60234-DAL **MANDARIN RUST**	DQE-60234-DAL **MANDARIN RUST**
DQE-21279-DAL **SAHARA TAN**	DQE-21279-DAL **SAHARA TAN**
DQE-21282-DAL **SPICE BROWN POLY.**	DQE-21282-DAL **SPICE BROWN POLY.**
DQE-21293-DAL **ADVENTURER GOLD POLY.**	DQE-21293-DAL **ADVENTURER GOLD POLY.**
DQE-8121-DAL **FROSTY WHITE**	DQE-8121-DAL **FROSTY WHITE**
DQE-11522-DAL **LIGHT AQUA**	DQE-11522-DAL **LIGHT AQUA**
DQE-70698-DAL **DUSTY ORANGE**	DQE-70698-DAL **DUSTY ORANGE**

DQE-41961-DAL
SAMOA GREEN

De Soto

2532	Sahara Tan*
2535	Hemlock Green Metallic*
2537	Dove Gray*
2624	Azure Blue Metallic*
82766	Summer Blue
82767	Sprout Greet
82768	Rye Beige
82769	Storm Charcoal Metallic
82770	Agate Green
82771	Golf Gray
82864	Honey Tan
82865	Amber
82866	Adventurer Buff

*De Soto exterior body colors, see 1957 De Soto Bulletin No. 14.

De Soto S-27

2540	Seatone Blue Metallic*
2541	Lagoon Blue*
2547	Sand Dune White**
2627	Leaf Green*
82734	Parrott Blue
82736	Sea Green
82737	Falstaff Green
82738	China Green
82740	Silver Gray Metallic
82741	African Gray
82742	Goldtone
82767	Sprout Green
82804	Oak Gray

*De Soto S-27 exterior body colors, see 1957 De Soto Bulletin No. 24.
** Plymouth exterior body color, see 1957 Plymouth Bulletin No. 25

New Color Information -Advance Bulletin 1-22-57

1957 DE SOTO
FIREDOME CODE S-25 and Fireflite CODE S-26

NEW COLOR

PAINT CODE	NAME	DITZLER CODE ENAMEL LACQUER DQE/DAL
PPP	Adventurer Gold Poly (Formerly known as Gold Tone Poly)	21273

Note: This color (21273) Is new and should not be mistaken with the color chip shown on the 1957 DeSoto color card which is a late 1956 color called Adventurer Gold Poly, 21293.

Additional Information on West Coast Colors
FIRESWEEP CODE S-27

LLL	FROSTY WHITE For cars built on west coast use Cloud White	8131 8036
NNN	Dusty Orange For cars built on west coast use Gauguin Red	70698 70693

New Color Information -Advance Bulletin 6-14-57

1957 DE SOTO SPRING COLOR

PAINT CODE	NAME	DITZLER CODE ENAMEL LACQUER DQE/DAL
VVV	Spanish Gold	21502

COLOR CHANGES

GGG	Charcoal Gray Poly *(Replace Charcoal Gray Poly 31321)*	31590

Production on the new color, 31590, will be started with cars showing the following serial numbers.

Firedome S-25	#55363489
Fireflite S-26	#50417646

JJJ	Muscatel Maroon Poly *(Replace Muscatel Maroon Poly 50448)*	50499

Production on the new color, 50499, will be started with cars showing the following serial numbers. West Coast Production will not be effected.

Firedome S-25	#55369010
Fireflite S-26	#50421930

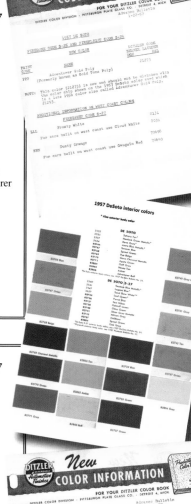

Grille Tech Sheet: 1957 Desoto Fireflite

Manufacturer: Desoto Division, Chrysler Motor Company
Body By: Chrysler
Designer: Virgil Exner
Assembly: Maywood Assembly Plant, Los Angeles, CA
Body Styles: 2-door Convertible, 2-door pillarless hardtop, 4-door sedan.
Production Numbers:

Fireflite S26

2-door hardtop	7,217
2-door convertible	1,151
4-door sedan	11,565
4-door hardtop	6,726
6-passenger station wagon	837
9-passenger station wagon	934
TOTAL PRODUCTION:	**28,430**

DRIVETRAIN

Engine: 341-cubic inch Hemi V-8. (4bbl Carter Carburetor)
Horsepower: 290@ 4600 RPM
Torque: 390 Ft. Lbs @ 2800 RPM
Transmission: Torque-Flite 3Spd Automatic
Drive Axle: 3.36:1 (standard) 3.18:1 or 3.54:1 optional
Wheelbase: 126"
Length: 218"
Width: 78.2"
Curb Weight: 4000 lbs.
MSRP: $3,485-$4,120 ($31,142 —$36,813 in 2018 dollars)

Current Values by Condition from Hagerty

2-door hardtop:
    #1 $56,600/ #2 $36,400/ #3 $27,400/#4 $16,400
4-door hardtop:
     #1 $27,900/#2 $19,000/#3 $14,500/$4 $10,500
Convertible:
    #1 $166,000/#2 $101,000/#3 $61,800/#4$ 45,100
2-door sedan:
    #1 $ 24,100/#2 $16,400/ #3 $12,600 /#4 $7,800
4-door 6-Pass. Wagon (Shopper):
    #1 $53,200/#2 $37,700/#3 $25,800/#4 $14,300
4-door 9-Pass. Wagon (Explorer):
    #1 $54,500/#2 $40,200/#3 $29,400/#4 $16,800

Front and back: The 1957 DeSoto Fireflite sported one of the era's boldest designs. But as impressive as the wide-mouth front grille was, the car's mammoth rear stacked tailfins stole the show. This two-door Sportsman Hardtop is owned by Phil Convertito of Stratford, CT.

Fast Facts

Did you know?

- The tail fins on the 1957 DeSoto Fireflite were not only eye-catching, they helped to stabilize the car at high speeds.
- In 1957 the Fireflite was superseded by the DeSoto Adventurer as the brand's top model. Nevertheless, Fireflites continued to offer high-grade appointments in a full line of body styles.
- The Fireflite's "Torqueflite" transmission was operated by a "Flite-Control" lever located on the dashboard.
- DeSoto added a station wagon to the Fireflite's lineup in 1957.
- Consumers loved DeSoto's new Forward Look styling, especially the massive fins with triple taillights and eagerly snapped up the cars. Overall sales jumped by 7,000 in 1957, which was no small feat in a recessionary auto market.
- This was DeSoto's last hurrah. Plagued by quality control issues, DeSoto's sales fell 60 percent in 1958, and Chrysler posted a loss of more than $40 million.
- Eager to stop the bleeding, Chrysler merged DeSoto with the new Chrysler-Plymouth division and stopped building DeSotos in a dedicated factory. It wasn't enough. DeSoto celebrated its 30th anniversary by selling just 45,700 cars. Its last car rolled off the assembly line in 1961.

Chapter 6:
1959 Dodge Custom Royal Lancer: Can Grilling Get More Ornate?

Of all the great grilles of the '50s, it would be hard to find one that was more ornate and menacing than the wrap-around bumper and grille guards on the 1959 Dodge Custom Royal Lancer.

Styling tweaks to the '59 made this the most curvaceous Lancer since Virgil Exner's startling "Forward Look" design was unveiled in the fall of 1956. And while the Lancer name had been a Dodge mainstay for decades, many Dodge aficionados consider this to be the most memorable of all Lancer models. If you count the car's recessed quad headlights and prominent eyebrows as part of the full front-end treatment (and it's hard not to), the visual impact is unmistakable more than six decades later.

In the mid-1950s, Exner was keen to shed the Dodge division's stodgy "old man" image. By 1959, Exner's Forward Look styling had firmly resolved that problem, and Dodge was looking to end the decade with a bang. The '59 Custom Royal Lancer succeeded beyond his wildest dreams. The Lancer's eyebrows over the headlights became larger and more pronounced.

To be fair, the front grille was only half of the car's styling appeal. The '59 carried over the big fins from 1957 and '58, although with slightly different profiles. The Forward Look's "Swept Wing" styling features (including the double-stacked rear tail lights and angular fins) made the Lancer appear as if it was perpetually in motion, even when the car was standing still. The '59's longer, lower, wider look only accentuated that perception.

Dodge's marketing machine wasn't shy about showing off the Lancer's front grille in advertising and in the division's dealer brochure (opposite page), press kit (left), as well as publicity photos (previous page).

Few would argue that the Lancer's heavily laden chrome front grille was one of the most complex of the era. It features a thick bumper that centers a stainless egg crate façade between a stylish Dodge grille topper. Above, bold parking lamps and quad headlights are highlighted by dramatic chrome eyebrows that flow into straight stainless belt moldings. They balance a planar profile with small wheel skirts, Lancer-specific fender emblems, rear-mounted louvers, and tucked and chrome-trimmed door handles.

The Lancer also sported some very sharp badging, including a distinctive late medieval Close Helmet logo set over a black background that also can be seen around the body, and even on the wheel cover centers.

MOPAR aficionados describe the car's styling as both "menacing" and "spectacular." Indeed, as you can see on the cover of Dodge's 1959 dealer brochure above, the front-end treatment makes the Lancer look like it's ready to eat a VW for lunch. If you're thinking of restoring one, however, bring lots of cash. Re-chroming the lower wraparound bumper, grille, and Dagmars will easily set you back about $5,000, provided they are in good condition.

Despite a curb weight of nearly 4,000 pounds, the Lancer had the power to move and move quickly.

As the horsepower race kicked into overdrive, Dodge made sure the Custom Royal Lancer had plenty of giddy up and go.

In 1957, the Custom Royal came from the factory with a standard four-barrel-topped 325-cubic inch block, dubbed the "Super Red Ram." Truly super, it produced 260hp and 335-lbs.ft. of torque from its 3.69 x 3.80-inch bore and stroke and 8.5:1 compression.

If that wasn't enough, Dodge offered higher power options, including the D-500, a 325-cubic inch block with Hemi cylinder heads and a 9.25 compression that developed 285hp and 345-lbs.ft. of torque. *Hemmings* reports that the Super D-500 option (technically the D-500-1), with its Hemi heads and dual quads, 310 horsepower and rated torque of 350-lbs.ft., was even more desirable.

An ultra-rare D-501 package offered performance-minded rag top owners a 340 horsepower 354-cubic inch Chrysler Hemi block borrowed from the record-setting 1956 Chrysler 300-B race cars.

The wraparound grille on the 1959 Dodge Custom Royal Lancer was one of the more complex and imposing front ends of the era, and a testament to the forward-looking designs of Virgil Exner.

As menacing as the front end was, the Lancer's "Swept Wing" style tail fins and double-stacked tail lights were (and continue to be) the real show stoppers on the '59 model.

"The D-501s were essentially purpose-built race cars offered to meet the homologation rules package; the AMA pulled its support from motorsports in mid-production," according to *Hemmings*. "As a result, the reported 100-odd engine/car combinations that were to be constructed were not finished. Today, only a few are known to exist out of a mere 56 (including three convertibles) that were built.

"In 1958, the Hemi block was eliminated and the new Ram Fire wedge engine became the base offering, producing 295 horsepower from its 350 cubic inches. Options included two variants of the 361-cubic inch engine – D-500 and Super D-500 – that, when coupled with a single or dual four-barrel carb, thundered 305 horsepower or 320 horsepower and 400 or 420-lbs.ft. of torque, respectively. Offered, and quickly recalled, was the Bendix Electrojector EFI version of the 361-cubic inch V-8 making 333 horsepower–all replaced by the dual-quad Super D-500. Collectors have a better shot at hitting the lottery than finding any part of the complicated EFI system.

"In the final year of the Custom Royal's existence, the D-500 offering of the previous year became the standard-issue V-8, assuming the Ram Fire name. The D-500 and Super D-500 V-8 options continued, but the engines measured out to 383 cubic inches, satisfying heavy right feet with 320 horsepower/420-lbs.ft. of torque when topped by a four-barrel, or 345 horsepower/425-lbs.ft. of torque when Super D-500 dual four-barrels were bolted onto the intake manifold."

The big Custom Royals will never be confused with drag racers, but they were some of the best performing cars on the road in 1959. In fact, all of the Dodges from that year had Torsion-Air front suspension and rear leaf springs. The convertibles had an X-brace to support the five cross members and boxed frame.

As popular as the Lancer's design was, sales suffered from a slumping national economy in 1958. Quality control issues, including a nasty tendency to rust, also didn't help. As a result, solid survivors are hard to come by, as are some replacement parts.

According to a 2006 article in *Hemmings Motor News*, two features found in the 1959 models also stand out. The first was optional swivel bucket seats. "Quite popular among the ladies, many found that they made ingress and egress significantly easier. Swivel buckets were a feature later installed on select GM models."

The second, the article added, was an all-new tri-color speedometer for 1959 that proved to be somewhat troublesome for colorblind drivers. "With no hand to follow, the gauge is divided into three segments and speed is indicated by color in each segment. Specifically, green is displayed to indicate speeds from 0 to 30 mph; it then changes to yellow until the vehicle hits 50 mph, when the indicator changes to red. *Motor Trend's* March 1959 test stated that, after dusk, the gauge is difficult to read."

Color-change gauge speedometers also were available on competing Oldsmobiles and Pontiacs through the early 1960s.

The 1959 Dodge Royal Custom Lancer is stunning in just about any two-tone color combination. This one sold new for $3,151.

1959 Dodge Colors

Paint Code		Paint Code	
BB-1	DQE-11813-DAL BLUE DIAMOND	**RR-1**	DQE-70791-DAL RUBY
CC-1	DQE-11812-DAL STAR SAPPHIRE POLY.	**UU-1**	DQE-21642-DAL BISCUIT
EE-1	DQE-42315-DAL AQUAMARINE	**WW-1**	DQE-21587-DAL MOCHA POLY.
FF-1	DQE-42295-DAL JADE POLY.	**XX-1**	DQE-8131-DAL PEARL
JJ-1	DQE-11720-DAL TURQUOISE	**YY-1**	DQE-81057-DAL CANARY DIAMOND
LL-1	DQE-31539-DAL SILVER POLY.	***JJJ**	DQE-11923-DAL FROSTED TURQUOISE POLY.
MM-1	DQE-31660-DAL PEWTER POLY.	***RRR**	DQE-70911-DAL POPPY
NN-1	DQE-70884-DAL ROSE QUARTZ	***TTT**	DQE-70923-DAL PARIS ROSE POLY.
PP-1	DQE-70885-DAL CORAL	**AA-1**	DQE-9000-DAL JET BLACK (NO SWATCH)

*1958 SPRING COLOR

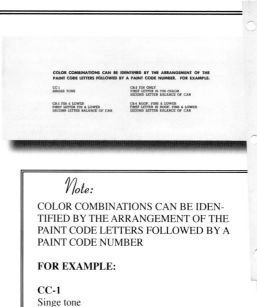

COLOR COMBINATIONS CAN BE IDENTIFIED BY THE ARRANGEMENT OF THE PAINT CODE LETTERS FOLLOWED BY A PAINT CODE NUMBER. FOR EXAMPLE:

CC-1
SINGLE TONE

CB-2 FIN ONLY
FIRST LETTER IS FIN COLOR
SECOND LETTER BALANCE OF CAR

CB-3 FIN & LOWER
FIRST LETTER IS FIN & LOWER
SECOND LETTER BALANCE OF CAR

CB-4 ROOF, FINS & LOWER
FIRST LETTER IS ROOF, FINS & LOWER
SECOND LETTER BALANCE OF CAR

Note:

COLOR COMBINATIONS CAN BE IDEN-
TIFIED BY THE ARRANGEMENT OF THE
PAINT CODE LETTERS FOLLOWED BY A
PAINT CODE NUMBER

FOR EXAMPLE:

CC-1
Singe tone

CB-2 Fin Only
First Letter is Fin Color.
Second Letter Balance of Car

CB-3 Fin & Lower
First Letter is Fin & Lower
Second Letter Balance of Car

CB-4 Roof, Fins, & Lower
First Letter is Roof, Fins & Lower
Second Letter Balance of Car

1959 Dodge interior colors

DITZLER COLOR DIVISION
PITTSBURGH PLATE GLASS COMPANY
Detroit 4, Michigan
Form 5902

SPECIFY { DAL– For DITZ-LAC® Automotive Lacquer
DQE– For DITZCO® Quickset Enamel

(Recreated for this publication for space and readability.)

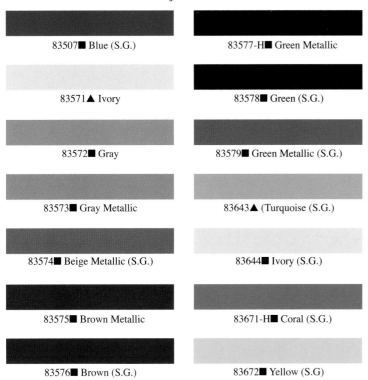

1959 Dodge Interior Colors

83507■ Blue (S.G.)	83577-H■ Green Metallic
83571▲ Ivory	83578■ Green (S.G.)
83572■ Gray	83579■ Green Metallic (S.G.)
83573■ Gray Metallic	83643▲ (Turquoise (S.G.)
83574■ Beige Metallic (S.G.)	83644■ Ivory (S.G.)
83575■ Brown Metallic	83671-H■ Coral (S.G.)
83576■ Brown (S.G.)	83672■ Yellow (S.G)

De Soto MS-1 and DODGE

	Color	Part No.
2539▲	Pearl White*	C-9101-B
3049■	Lake Blue Metallic*	C-2209-B
3056■	Forest Green Metallic*	C-3231-B
83570■	Lake Blue	C-2209-SB
83571▲	Glaze Ivory	C-9129-B
83572■	Wagon Gray	C-5162-B
83573■	Silver Gray Metallic	C-5148-B
83574■	Terra Beige Metallic	C-8851-SB
83575■	Sierra Brown Metallic	C-4101-B
83576■	Sierra Brown	C-4101-SB
83577-H■	Mallard Green Metallic	C-3200-B
83578■	Mallard Green	C-3200-B
83579■	Forest Green Metallic	C-3231-SB
83643▲	Turquoise	C-3235-SB
83644■	Glaze Ivory	C-9129-SB
83671-H■	Coral	C-7082-SB
83672■	Canary Yellow	C-9132-SB

*Also an exterior color

Grille Tech Sheet: 1959 Dodge Custom Royal Lancer

Manufacturer: Chrysler Corporation, Dodge Division.
Body by: Chrysler
1959 model year production: MD3-H: Custom Royal V8

- 2-door hardtop: 6,278
- 4-door hardtop: 5,019
- 2-door convertible: 984
- TOTAL: 21,206

NOTE: ONLY HARDTOP MODELS WERE LABELED LANCER

Engine: Dodge offered five different V-8 configurations for the Lancer:

1. V8 326-cubic inch 255 HP@ 4400 RPM/with 2bbl Carb 335-ft.lbs.torque (Super Red Ram)

2. V8 361-cubic inch 295 HP @ 4600 RPM/with 2bbl Carb (Ram Fire) 350-ft. lbs torque

3. V8 361-cubic inch 305 HP @ 4600 RPM/with Carter 4bbl Carb (Ram Fire) 400-ft.lbs torque

4. V8 383-cubic inch 320 HP @ 4600 RPM/with 4bbl Carter Carb 420-ft.lbs. torque (D-500)

5. V8 383-cubic inch 345 HP @ 5000 RPM/with Dual 4bbl Carter Carb 425-ft.lbs torque (Super D-500)

Transmission: 3-speed automatic Torque-Flite with pushbutton shift.
Wheelbase: 122 Inches.
Differential: Since all Royal Lancers for 1959 have the 3-speed automatic transmission, final drive was just one ratio, 2.93:1
Curb Weight: Conv: 3,990 lbs. 2-door HT 4,030 lbs. 4-door Hardtop 3,870 lbs.
MSRP: $3,150-$4,000 ($27,250-$34,599 in 2018 dollars)

Current Values from Hagerty:
Custom Royal Lancer 2-door HT 383 V8 4BBL:
    #1 $70,400 /#2 $43,100/#3 $28,700/#4 $17,000
Custom Royal Lancer 4-door HT 383 V8 4BBL:
    #1 $30,000/#2 $22,200/#3 $15,200/#4 $10,001
Custom Royal Lancer Convertible 383 V8 2x 4BBL (<1000made)
    #1 $155,000 /#2$111,000/#3 $66,700/ #4 $45,800
Custom Royal 4dr Post Sedan 383 V8 4BBL:
    #1 $25,100/#2 $20,200/#3 $13,300/#4 $8,500

Fast Facts

Did you know?

- Though Dodge was often second in the marketing pecking order for Chrysler, the 1959 Dodge Custom Royal Lancer with its exaggerated styling and extravagant name commanded attention when it debuted. It has been called the "glitter queen" of the "Forward Look."
- The 1959 Dodge Custom Royal Lancer was longer, lower, and wider than any previous Dodge.
- Outside, the car was layered in chrome, from the full-length body side moldings, to the shiny fin edges, to the huge big-mouth grille and twin-headlight arrangement.
- Though they featured a slate of powerful Chrysler V-8s, the Custom Royals were too big to be drag racers or economy cars. But they were regarded as some of the best performing cars on the road in 1959.
- On V8 powered models, a V8 emblem was customized to the side, just below the V in the side trim.
- For a big, heavy car, the Royal Lancer could move, but performance varied depending on the engine size. Simulation tests with the top of the line 383 cubic inch V-8 claim the car could do 0-60 mph in under 10 seconds. Royal Lancers equipped with smaller V-6 engines took their time – up to 14 seconds.
- Fuel economy at 10.9 mpg was more in line with a car that weighed 3,860 pounds. But that could vary with engine size and ranges running anywhere from 12 -17 mpg.
- The '59 Dodge was a couple of steps removed, stylistically, from the clean, sweeping designs of Virgil Exner's '57 Chrysler cars, and the exaggerated design features (or "gorp" as some automotive reviewers called them) were noticed on the Lancer.
- In 1959 it was not unusually to see complete annual styling makeovers. Exner had also suffered a debilitating heart attack soon after he'd designed Chrysler's groundbreaking 1957 models, and wasn't able to further influence the designs for the "Forward Look" sequels.
- Although everything at Dodge was billed as brand new in 1959, it also marked the end of an era; the final model year for body-on frame construction. The new 1960 Dodge models would introduce a new "Unibody" design.

Opposite page: Oldsmobile's 1953 Fiesta in multiple two-tone color combinations offered one of the era's more iconic front grilles. The limited production special edition car was made specifically to celebrate GM's 50th anniversary and was a one-year hit at GM's annual Motorama Show.

Chapter 7:
A Fiesta Grille Worth Celebrating

Ask any Oldsmobile aficionado to list the most historic Oldsmobiles of all time, and the 1953 Fiesta would be right at the top, along with Ransom Eli Olds' 1901 Curved Dash, the rocket powered 1950 '88, which ushered in the muscle car era, and the front-wheel drive 1966 Toronado.

What makes the '53 Fiesta different is that it was one of three top-of-the-line convertibles developed under the watchful eye of Harley Earl to commemorate GM's 50th anniversary. The Fiesta, along with the Cadillac Eldorado and Buick Skylark, were the Triple Crown show pieces of GM's celebrated Motorama show in 1953. The Buick was the sportiest of the three. The Eldorado was the toniest (what else?). And the Fiesta was Oldsmobile's version of a luxury boulevard car.

All three "dream cars" were based on GM's C-Body shell and previewed forthcoming design ideas. The Fiesta hinted at what was yet to come in 1954, with its "hockey stick" side trim and wraparound panoramic windshield a year before it went into regular production.

Unlike the Eldorado and Skylark, the Fiesta had regular body contours, but it was loaded with just about every factory option you could find and some that weren't available anywhere else, such as a specially tuned 170-horsepower version of Oldsmobile's 303-cubic-inch Rocket V-8 engine. Even though it offered five horsepower more than traditional 98s, it couldn't offset the car's additional 350 pounds. But it helped add more sizzle to the steak.

The Fiesta was never short on sizzle. The car featured colorful two-tone paint finishes, a self-shifting (automatic) Hydra-Matic transmission, power steering and brakes, custom leather upholstery, Autronic Eye headlight dimmer, backup lights, power-operated brakes and steering, hydraulic power windows and front seat, a heater/defroster, Super Deluxe radio, whitewall tires, and flipper hubcaps.

Initially, Olds offered just four color combinations: Solid black, solid white, Noel Green with Nile Green, and Surf Blue with Teal Blue. Additional color combinations were added to the catalog later in the year. Interiors were either light green, light blue or black buffed leather, trimmed with ivory leather. Although the engine was Olds' regular 303-cubic inch Rocket V-8, the Fiesta had 8.3:1 compression and a single Rochester 4GC carburetor.

The Fiesta shared a common chromed front grille with the rest of the Olds lineup. And it wasn't all that different from the droopy or frowning front grilles that debuted on the 1949 Oldsmobile 88 and had been evolving ever since. The Fiesta's three-part grille featured a curved upper lip that molded below the hood line and wrapped around the side fenders. The lower half of the front bumper housed two massive Dagmars connected by a horizontal bar in the center grille area. It also wrapped around the sides of the car, giving the appearance of a lower lip.

Together, the entire grille assembly, including upper, lower and Dagmar bullets, weighs in at more than 100 pounds. Collectively, they create a visual smorgasbord of chrome that provoked no shortage of opinions about the Fiesta in the day. What's sad looking to some is considered stately to others. Harley Earl was particularly enamored with the look, so it stuck. But the frown eventually softened in 1955, giving Olds a more refined and less serious front end. In 1956, the Dagmars disappeared entirely, creating a large gaping grille derived from a 1953 Olds Starfire convertible concept car that never went into production. By then, the Olds grille was fairly sedate compared to Cadillacs and Chryslers, and many referred to it as the "catfish grille."

This 1953 Fiesta, which graces the front cover of this book, was restored by Mike Fusick, owner of Fusick Automotive Inc., in East Windsor, Connecticut.

OLDSMOBILE'S FABULOUS NEW *Fiesta*

A Custom Classic with a festive flair! It's Fiesta—the merriest, most magnificent Oldsmobile ever built—with low-sweeping silhouette, panoramic windshield . . . a galaxy of glamour features! For the discriminating motorist—*it's the sports car supreme!*

NEW SUPER

CONVERTIBLE COUPÉ

Power Styling at its peak! All outdoors is yours in this sleek new Convertible Coupé! Deep-buffed leather interiors in striking colors provide the ultimate in cruising luxury.

The 1953 Fiesta (top left) featured the same front grille as the rest of Oldsmobile's lineup. Though the Fiesta offered some unique features and plenty of bells and whistles, in dealer brochures it was hard to tell it apart from the standard 98 convertible or base 88 convertible (top right).

Priced from $5,715, just 458 of the Motorama-inspired Fiestas were produced beginning in mid-1953, and few have survived. Many consider the Fiesta the rarest of the three among postwar Oldsmobiles, and an extremely rare sight at car shows. In 1953, demand for the Fiesta wasn't what Olds had hoped, as many prospective buyers figured out they could get pretty much the same car in a standard 98 convertible for nearly half the price.

Olds collectors are quick to note the differences between the Fiesta and a standard 98. In addition to the panoramic windshield and custom two-tone colors, the Fiesta featured tri-bar spinner hubcaps, a chrome trunk strip, and slightly more horsepower under the hood.

But collectors have been much kinder to the Fiesta, based largely on its prominence as a Motorama car. At one point, market values escalated to more than $200,000. Prices have since slid back to the $125,000 range, although a Fiesta in No. 1 condition can still be valued at more than $200,000.

Top and opposite page, lower left: A 1953 Olds 98 Convertible owned by Don Jack in Stratford, CT., sports a front grille treatment that is identical to the Fiesta's.

Grille Tech Sheet: 1953 Oldsmobile Fiesta Convertible
Manufacturer: Oldsmobile Division, General Motors Corp.
Body by: Fisher Body Division, General Motors

1953 model year production 458
Engine: 304-cubic inch (5.0L) "Rocket" V8
The 170 HP is 5 HP more than the standard 304 engine, achieved by increasing compression to 8.3:1 vs 8:1 in the standard engine.
    Available only with Fiesta Convertible.
Horsepower/Torque: 170 HP/290 ft. lbs @ 3600 RPM
Transmission: 4-Speed Hydra-Matic "Super Drive" Automatic
Wheelbase: 124 Inches
Curb Weight: 4,459 lbs. (336 more lbs than Std. 98 Cvt)
MSRP: $5,719, nearly twice the price of the standard 98 convertible at $2,963 ($53,915 in 2019 dollars)

Production Colors: Only four color choices were initially offered by Oldsmobile. Additional combinations were later added.
    Two-Tone Options: Noel Green Body/Nile Green rear deck and Surf Blue body/Teal Blue rear deck.
    Solid Color options: Polar White and Black
    "The two-tone effect is obtained by painting the rear deck and the top of both rear fenders above the chrome trim a
        darker color than the rest of the car."
Source: *"News from Oldsmobile"* 4/20/1953

Interior Colors/Material
"Contrasting with the body colors are three hand buffed leather upholstery options. The seats, seat backs and lower door panels
    are finished in dark colored leather with ivory leather trim around the seat edges, tops and upper door panels."
Source: "News from Oldsmobile"

Solid Color Fiestas: Ivory Leather/Black Leather
Two Tone Green Fiesta: Light Green Metallic Leather/Ivory Leather
Two Tone Blue Fiesta: Light Blue Metallic Leather/Ivory Leather
Two Tone Raven Red: Raven Red and White

****Instrument Panel and Steering color match upholstery colors****

Current Values from Hagerty:
    #1 $208,000/#2 $152,000/#3 $129,000/#4 $98,700

This plush Olds 98 had distinctive styling features. It came with all the same features as on the less expensive models, plus standard extras including a padded dash, full wheel discs, windshield washers and deluxe steering wheel. The engine was a hot four-barrel version. Cloth or leather upholstery choices were offered. Most Olds owners paid $132 extra to have Hydra-Matic Drive. The production of the Holiday Coupes was 27,920.

1953 Oldsmobile 98 Holiday Coupe
FP: $3022
Weight: 3893 lbs.
Engine: V-8
DISP: 303.7 CID
WB: 124 in.
Tires: 7.60 x 15
B X S : 3 3/4 x 3-7.16 in.
HP: 165 @ 3600 RPM

Top right and right: This stunning '53 Olds Fiesta is #438 of 458 made. It is owned by Leo & Karen Stutzman of Brandon, FL. Photos by Jeff Walsh taken at the 2019 Olds National Show in Wichita, KS.

Fast Facts

Did you know?

- The 1953 Fiesta, one of three limited edition "futuristic dream cars" featured in GM's 50th Anniversary Motorama show, was the most expensive Oldsmobile, and more than twice the price of the top-of-the-line, full-size '98.
- The Fiesta bucked auto industry tradition and was introduced mid-year specifically for the auto show circuit.
- Though it was a one-year model, it offered a styling preview for the next generation of Oldsmobiles with features that later became standard throughout the Olds lineup.
- The Fiesta would only last one year, but the name was revived in 1957 on Oldsmobile station wagons.
- The Fiesta's most distinguishing feature was its Panoramic Windshield, which was developed by GM design vice president Harley Earl in partnership with glassmaker Libbey-Owens-Ford (L-O-F). Earl reportedly strong-armed L-O-F, which insisted that Plexiglass technology of the day wasn't ready for the radical wraparound curves. Earl prevailed and Panoramic Windshields became standard on 1954 Olds models, and eventually the entire GM lineup.
- The windshields not only looked stylish, they also made the Fiesta appear lower than traditional 98 models.
- The Fiesta shared with Cadillac a Super DeLuxe signal-seeking radio, with a power antenna that could be operated by a foot button on the driver's side floor near the dimmer switch.
- Many assume that all Fiestas were orange-and-white, because pictures of those models are the most common. But the orange color used on the Fiesta is really called Raven Red. According to *Collectible Automobile Magazine*, about half of the surviving Fiestas are turquoise and white, and several other all-black and all-white examples are known.
- More color combinations were offered for the Fiesta than its Motorama cousins, which led to speculation over the years that Oldsmobile had planned to produce more Fiestas than it actually did.
- Auto customizers loved the Fiesta's spinner wheel covers. When driven slowly, their triple flippers put on a show. Accessory houses quickly offered knockoffs and modified versions, which are still referred to as "Fiesta spinners."
- The Fiesta's pedigree as a future collectible was not as obvious in 1953 as it might seem. Most changed hands quickly and went through several owners, which explains the low survival rate.
- Arthur Godfrey, the popular radio and television show host, was the only known celebrity owner.

Chapter 8

1952 Pontiac Chieftain: Last of the Old School Cool

For Pontiac buffs and automotive historians, the 1952 Pontiac Chieftain is considered a crossover of sorts. It combines the last of the old-school, pre-war curves with a hint of the power and performance that was yet to come in the second half of the decade.

The Chieftain's wrap-around front grille would certainly qualify on both counts. With five (count 'em) horizontal bars, two vertical cross-members and two curved bumper protectors, the Chieftain sports enough lines and spaces to comfortably compose a musical score. Add in the chrome, which Pontiac poured on in spades later in the decade under automotive maverick Semon E. "Bunkie" Knudsen, and there's little question that the design of the '52 Chieftain grille was a generational crossover for Detroit.

Of course, no self-respecting automotive reviewer would claim that the Chieftain's front grille was the most outstanding feature on Pontiacs of this era. That honor goes to the lighted amber Indian head ornament that adorned the hoods of early decade Chieftains and Chieftain Catalinas. Lit at night, the amber hood ornaments are true show stealers. (The same can be said during daylight hours even when the lights aren't on.) So we won't overlook or avoid the obvious here. Suffice it to say, there's little doubt the Chieftain's hood ornament is a big part of the front end's charm.

At the same time, it's hard to believe that early decade Chieftains were viewed as "old man's cars." When compared to the lower, wide-track Pontiacs that followed, the contrast is apparent, and prices are reflected accordingly in today's collector car market. That's why Chieftains from the early to mid-'50s are often politely referred to as "affordable" alternatives to the more youthful and desirable Pontiacs that followed.

Even still, Pontiac sold a ton of Chieftains in 1952. Though the brand finished fifth in automotive sales, Pontiac sold more than 271,000 Chieftains. Prospective buyers found a lot to like when the '52 models hit showroom floors in the fall of 1951. Besides the front grille and Indian head hood ornament, the Chieftain featured dual chrome hood stripes that ran from the cowl lacing to the front grille, giving the appearance that Chief Pontiac had a front-row seat overlooking a cascading chrome waterfall. (Knudsen was not a fan, and often called the chrome stripes "old men's suspenders." They disappeared in 1957.)

From the side, twin arrowhead ("Silver Streak") shaped chrome strips run from the front of the car to the back and matching Indian head emblems were embedded in the rear fenders to finish off the treatment.

Pontiac's fascination with chrome extended to the interior of the car as well. One review in *Hemming's Classic Car* characterized the treatment like this: "Extensive use of chrome made the Chieftain's interior look more like a Wurlitzer organ than an automotive dashboard. A semicircular speedometer was directly in front of the driver, with four gauges below. On the right, a small panel housed the heater and radio controls."

Back in the day, Chieftains traditionally were considered solid and reliable cars – not a whole lot different from Howard Cunningham's DeSoto in *Happy Days*. Much of that can be credited to the

The front grille on the 1952 Pontiac Chieftain has enough lines to compose a musical score. But even with all that chrome, the real show-stealer on this car has always been the amber Pontiac Indian Chief hood ornament.

Above and below: '52 Pontiac Chieftain Deluxe owned by Howard Slater of Buxton, Maine.

A Great <u>Dual-Range</u> Performer
with Spectacular <u>Power</u> and <u>Economy</u>!

PONTIAC MOTOR DIVISION OF GENERAL MOTORS CORPORATION

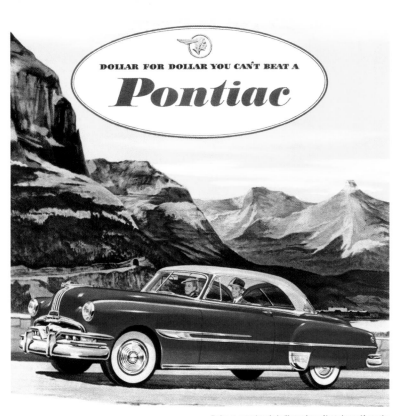

On the open road—or in city traffic
Dual-Range Performance gives you driving at its best!

PONTIAC MOTOR DIVISION OF GENERAL MOTORS CORPORATION

Pontiac's advertising heralded the Chieftain's new Dual-Range Automatic transmission and affordable performance capabilities.
Ads courtesy of the Automotive History Preservation Society.

Dollar for Dollar you can't beat the '52 *Pontiac* ... Built to last 100,000 Miles!

No car on the road has a better record for dependability and long-range economy than Pontiac. With only routine maintenance, Pontiac has proved—year in and year out—its ability to cover thousands upon thousands of miles with remarkable freedom from repairs. Pontiac is a sound long-term investment—"Built to Last 100,000 Miles." The records prove it over and over.

Chieftain De Luxe Four-Door Sedan
COLOR SHOWN: POTOMAC BLUE UPPER, MAYFLOWER BLUE LOWER

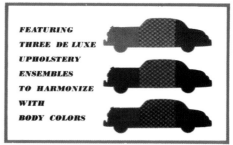

FEATURING THREE DE LUXE UPHOLSTERY ENSEMBLES TO HARMONIZE WITH BODY COLORS

Chieftain De Luxe Two-Door Sedan
COLOR SHOWN: SMOKE GREY UPPER, SHELL GRAY LOWER

Chieftain De Luxe Convertible
COLOR SHOWN: CHEROKEE RED

The Pontiac Steel Station Wagon
COLOR SHOWN: FOREST GREEN

Sedan Delivery
COLOR SHOWN: SATURN GOLD

White sidewall tires at extra cost when available.

Ads courtesy of the Automotive History Preservation Society.

Presenting the '52 **Pontiac**

with Spectacular New *Dual–Range* Performance!

DOLLAR FOR DOLLAR YOU CAN'T BEAT A PONTIAC

Equipment, accessories and trim illustrated are subject to change without notice.

Featuring a Wonderful New Power Train

1 <u>More</u> <u>Powerful</u> High-Compression Engine

2 Wonderful <u>Dual-Range</u> Hydra-Matic Drive*

3 New High-Performance Economy Axle

THE POWER YOU WANT   WHEN YOU   WANT IT   WHERE YOU WANT IT

THE great 1952 Pontiac is so *new* and *different* in its performance that only a ride can tell you what it's like! First of all, it brings you General Motors' sensational new Dual-Range Hydra-Matic Drive.* Pontiac is not only the *first* car to bring you this amazing development —*but it is the lowest-priced car to offer it for 1952!*

Coupled with this wonderful advancement is Pontiac's great high-compression engine—plus a new high-performance, economy axle. These three great developments combine to form a "power train" that actually delivers "tailor-made" performance. At the *touch of your finger*, you can elect to have tremendous acceleration and snap and go! Or, with equal ease, you can choose an altogether *different* type of performance: silken, gliding, gas-saving—perfection itself for the open road.

Truly, it's a never-ending sensation to order the *power you want—when* you want it—and *where* you want it. And there are many *other* advancements in the new Pontiac, too. Better *see* it—and *drive* it—today!

Optional at extra cost.

PONTIAC MOTOR DIVISION OF GENERAL MOTORS CORPORATION

introduction of GM's all-new four-speed automatic Dual Range Hydra-Matic transmission, which represented a significant improvement over previous models. Pontiac advertising showcased the transmission as a "Great Dual-Range Performer with Spectacular Power and Economy!" Early adopters responded to the pitch.

Two engine versions were offered in 1952 – a straight-six or straight-eight. These naturally balanced power plants had a creamy smoothness usually reserved for luxury cars, and they really helped Pontiac transcend its budget-minded market placement. Pontiac's 268 cubic-inch straight-eight motor earned a reputation for being smooth, reliable and quite sturdy. The base six-cylinder was a 239.2-cu.in. L-head straight-six, with a 3-9/16-inch bore and a 4-inch stroke. With its Rochester BC one-barrel carburetor, it developed 100 horsepower at 3,400 rpm when used with a manual transmission.

The larger straight-eight engine came in two horsepower variations – a 118 horsepower version for the manual transmission and 122 horsepower version with the automatic transmission.

Both power plants were well known for reliability and longevity, "thanks mainly to their use of full-pressure lubrication, including rifle-drilled connecting rods for positive wrist-pin lubrication," according to *Hemmings*.

Grille Tech Sheet: 1952 Pontiac Chieftain
Manufacturer: Pontiac Division, General Motors
Body by: Fisher Body Division, General Motors
Assembly Point: Pontiac, MI
Some models: South Gate, CA; Arlington, TX; Wilmington, DE; Atlanta, GA
Kansas City, KS; Framingham, MA; and Linden, NJ.
1952 model year production: 271,373
    Series 25 (6-cyl.) 19,809
    Series 27 (8-cyl.) 251,564
Body Options:
    2-door sedan
    4-door sedan
    2-door coupe
    2-door hardtop
    2-door convertible
    4-door station wagon
Engine:
- 239 C.I Inline 6 cyl. 103HP/189 ft. lbs. Torque @ 3000 RPM with Hydra-Matic /194 ft. lbs.
- 268 C.I Inline 8 cyl. 121HP/ 222 ft. lbs. Torque @ 3000 RPM with Hydra-Matic/ 227 ft. lbs.

Wheelbase: 122 inches
Curb Weight: Range of 3448 lbs-3728 lbs
MSRP: $2,090 for Base Model ($19,935.92 in 2019 Dollars)
Current Values from Hagerty:
    2-door sedan: #1 $28,800/#2 $18,800/#3 $10,600/#4 $8,200
    4-door sedan: #1 $17,600/#2 $12,800/#3 $7300/#4 $4,700
    4-door wagon: #1 $78,900/#2 $53,700/#3 $41,100/#4 $33,600
    2-door hardtop: #1 $30,500/#2 $20,700/#3 $ 10,900/#4 $8,300
    2-door convertible: #1 $45,000/#2 $32,800/#3 $16,400/#4 $10,800

1952 Pontiac Chieftain Interior Colors

Chieftains and Chieftain Catalinas had multiple options in interior colors and materials.

- Full leather was available in black, blue, green, red or tan.

- Mixed leather interiors were available in three material types: "Cloth," "Fabric" and "Pile" configurations.

- Material colors were available in grey, black, red, dark green, pale green.

- The less expensive Chieftain two- and four-door post Sedans had three all-cloth options, a plain color and check pattern in dark blue, dark green and dark grey.

- An "Imitation Leather" option was also available in tan and dark grey for the station wagon.

1952 Pontiac Chieftain Colors

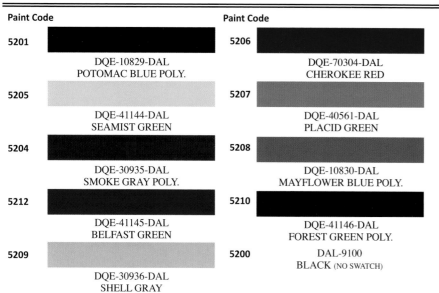

Paint Code

5201
DQE-10829-DAL
POTOMAC BLUE POLY.

5205
DQE-41144-DAL
SEAMIST GREEN

5204
DQE-30935-DAL
SMOKE GRAY POLY.

5212
DQE-41145-DAL
BELFAST GREEN

5209
DQE-30936-DAL
SHELL GRAY

Paint Code

5206
DQE-70304-DAL
CHEROKEE RED

5207
DQE-40561-DAL
PLACID GREEN

5208
DQE-10830-DAL
MAYFLOWER BLUE POLY.

5210
DQE-41146-DAL
FOREST GREEN POLY.

5200
DAL-9100
BLACK (NO SWATCH)

Paint Code   SEE 1950-1951 COLOR CARD FORM 5107 FOR COLOR CHIPS ON THE FOLLOWING COLORS.

5203
DQE-50229-DAL
VICTORIA MAROON POLY.

5211
DQE-20780-DYL
SATURN GOLD SYMPO

5224
DQE-20696-DAL
LIDO BEIGE

5125 (A)
DQE-50231-DAL
IMPERIAL MAROON

5125 (B)
DQE-30680-DAL
SAND GRAY POLY.

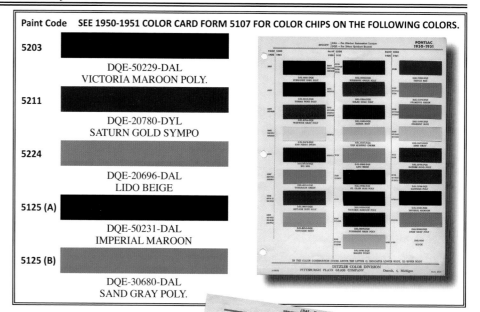

TWO-TONE COMBINATIONS

5214	(U)	DQE-30935-DAL	SMOKE GRAY POLY.
	(L)	DQE-30936-DAL	SHELL GRAY
5215	(U)	DQE-41145-DAL	BELFAST GREEN
	(L)	DQE-41144-DAL	SEAMIST GREEN
5217	(U)	DQE-41146-DAL	FOREST GREEN POLY.
	(L)	DQE-40561-DAL	PLACID GREEN
5219	(U)	DQE-10830-DAL	MAYFLOWER BLUE POLY.
	(L)	DQE-30936-DAL	SHELL GRAY
5222	(U)	DQE-41144-DAL	SEAMIST GREEN
	(L)	DQE-41145-DAL	BELFAST GREEN
5229	(U)	DQE-10829-DAL	POTOMAC BLUE POLY.
	(L)	DQE-10830-DAL	MAYFLOWER BLUE POLY.

U = UPPER BODY
L= LOWER BODY

STATION WAGON COLORS

5223	(BC)	DQE-41146-DAL	FOREST GREEN POLY.
	(PI)	DQE-40561-DAL	PLACID GREEN
5224	(BC)	DQE-20780-DYL	SATURN GOLD SYMPO
	(PI)	DQE-20696-DAL	LIDO BEIGE
5225	(BC)	DQE-50231-DAL	IMPERIAL MAROON
	(PI)	DQE-30680-DAL	SAND GRAY POLY
5226	(BC)	DQE-40561-DAL	PLACID GREEN
	(PI)	DQE-41146-DAL	FOREST GREEN POLY.

BC = BODY COLOR
PI = PANEL INSERT

SPECIFY
{
DAL– For DITZ-LAC® Automotive Lacquer
DQE– For DITZCO® Quickset Enamel
DYL– For Sympho-Chromatic Lacquer
}

DITZLER COLOR DIVISION
PITTSBURGH PLATE GLASS COMPANY
Detroit 4, Michigan
Form 5207

(Recreated for this publication for space and readability.)

Fast Facts

Did you know?

- Following World War II, the Pontiac Chieftain was one of the first cars to offer consumers the appeal of a full-bodied sports car minus the often prohibitive costs associated with convertibles.
- In the May 1952 issue of *Popular Mechanics*, the Chieftain did 0-60 mph in 14.9 seconds– no great shakes by today's standards, but pretty quick for its day.
- The '52 Chieftain's dash takes its cues from early jet-age cockpits, with a giant aviation-inspired radio speaker grille and inset clock in the center, and a neatly stacked and well-divided cluster of gauges directly in front of the driver.
- The Chieftain's design was such a hit that it served as the basis for mid-line Catalinas and higher-end Bonnevilles later in the decade.
- Pontiac offered four Chieftain station wagons for 1952: two each in the Chieftain Six and Eight cylinder series. A top-line, Chieftain Eight, Deluxe six passenger woody wagon carried a starting sticker price of $2,772. Among the most unique of its many accessories are the picnic cooler and jug, and the pocketbook holder. Few survivors remain today.
- The Chieftain was not a must-have and be-seen car for celebrities. The closest we could find was Jack Benny, who nurtured his frugally cheap image in a '51 Chieftain.
- But it's not hard to find '52 Chieftains at the movies. You'll find them in *Simon Birch, The Intruder, James Dean, Cribs, The Great St. Louis Train Robbery, Funny Face, Quantum Leap* and *Not as a Stranger*. On TV, if you look closely, you'll see a '52 Chieftain make a brief appearance in an episode of *Mod Squad* in the late 1960s.

Opposite page: Pontiac's signature split-grille still shines on this 1959 Bonneville that we found waiting to get some TLC at Peluso's Precision Automotive in Mendon, Mass., which specializes in classic Pontiac repairs and restorations. The driver's side cove featured the Bonneville script logo. Both grilles framed an arching waterfall-styled hood ornament that paid homage to earlier Pontiac hood treatments. From just about any angle, there is little doubt that the first Wide Track Pontiac lived up to its name.

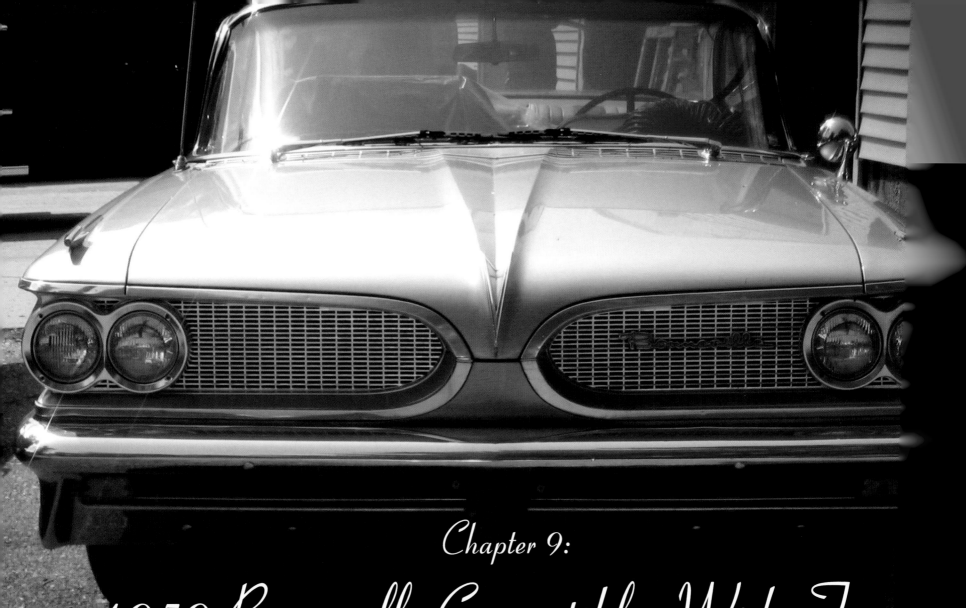

Chapter 9:

1959 Bonneville Convertible: Wide Track with Plenty of Room for the Grille

Who in the World Built this Beauty...
the only car with
Wide-Track Wheels?

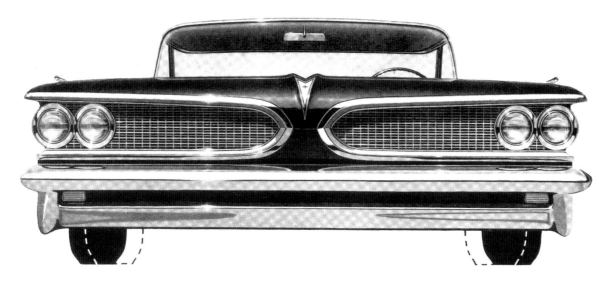

EXCLUSIVELY YOURS—*WIDE-TRACK* WHEELS

Wheels moved out a full 5 inches for the widest, steadiest stance in America—better cooling for engine and brakes—lower center of gravity for better grip on the road, safer cornering, smoother ride, easier handling. *You get the most beautiful roadability in the whole wide world!*

On Display Oct. 9th

The 1959 Bonneville ushered in a new design era for Pontiac that featured "Strato-Styling," "Wide Track" wheels, and a distinctive signature split-grille. Never shy about touting the obvious, Pontiac's advertising "stretched" the truth just a tad with illustrations like this one that intentionally made the front-end look even wider than it actually was. Ad courtesy of the Automotive History Preservation Society.

At age 14, Semon E. "Bunkie" Knudsen asked his father, legendary GM President and automotive maverick William "Big Bill" Knudsen, for a car. His father agreed, but there was a catch: The car was in hundreds of pieces, and Bunkie had to assemble it. He did.

In 1939, Bunkie Knudsen arrived at GM as the boss's son, with a master's degree from the Massachusetts Institute of Technology. His nickname? Bestowed on him by his father, it was a World War I term short for "bunkmates," or close friends.

Big Bill was Henry Ford's production boss when he accepted Alfred P. Sloan's invitation to join GM and Chevrolet in 1921. The elder Knudsen was GM's president from 1937 to 1940, when he left to run the nation's war production machinery, and it appeared at the time that Bunkie would be destined to follow his father's steps to the presidency.

Bunkie worked hard to learn the trade and became general manager of GM's Detroit Diesel Engine Division in 1955. It was the first of several major promotions. A year later, he was given control of Pontiac, which wasn't exactly a dream assignment because Pontiac was widely regarded as an "old man's car."

Bunkie saw the division as the weakest link in GM's brand juggernaut, a perennial fifth-place performer, that needed to carve out a niche of its own. So he made it his first priority as general manager to change that image. Knudsen was astute enough to know that merely selling Pontiacs as upgraded Chevrolets would never work. He knew the key to jump-starting the brand was to appeal to youthful buyers and often said, "You can sell a young man's car to an old man, but you can't sell an old man's car to a young man."

What GM lacked in its marketing arsenal was a performance brand. Pontiacs, Knudsen decided, would become sporty.

Just before production of the 1957 models began, Bunkie ordered the designers to remove the trademark silver streak that had adorned many Pontiac hoods since 1935. He was told it was too late. But Knudsen insisted, and the 1957 Pontiac was built without the silver streak.

He defied an auto-industry gentlemen's agreement banning racing and committed Pontiac to factory-backed NASCAR and NHRA teams. These soon enjoyed huge success on the racing circuits, thanks largely to the brand's newly developed V-8. He also surrounded himself with a team of hard-core performance enthusiasts, including a young John De Lorean as the director of advanced engineering, and ad man and drag racer Jim Wangers. Both became instrumental in shaping Pontiac's performance-driven image in the 1960s.

In 1956, Pete Estes joined Pontiac from Oldsmobile as chief engineer. The Knudsen-Estes-DeLorean team began reshaping Pontiac's cars and its image quickly.

The effort really kicked into high gear with a true sense of urgency in 1957. After getting an eyeful of Chrysler's new "Forward Look" designs, Bunkie ordered a complete makeover that would give Pontiac's lineup a distinctive new look and performance image beginning with the 1959 model year.

True to his word, he changed everything. Look-alike Chevys, Indian head hood ornaments and silver streaks were out. The Chieftain and Super Chief names were retired, and the Catalina, which was previously used only on two-door hardtops, graduated to a series.

Knudsen also introduced the Bonneville in 1957, a new top-of-the-line model with a racing-inspired name, to attract younger buyers, and to take aim at Chrysler, which had leap-frogged GM in styling and performance gains in the latter half of the decade.

For '59, Pontiac offered three model lines – the entry-level Catalina, a mid-priced Star Chief, and the top-tier Bonneville (with additional body styles).

For the first time, the front-end sported a signature split-grille. Though less performance-oriented, the split-grille theme took a brief hiatus in 1960 and returned in 1961 to become a defining styling element on most Pontiacs until the division's demise in 2010.

The upper portion of the grille was separated by twin coves that surrounded and framed the car's headlights. The twin-cove styling feature resonated with Detroit design stylists in different ways. GM used the same side-by-side design a year later on Oldsmobile dash boards. And Ford later adapted the look on early Mustangs in 1964.

The lower portion of the grille, which splits into two pieces, wraps around the front of the car, providing a polished chrome frame that houses the turn signals and parking lights.

From the front, the entire grille assembly literally looks like it's a mile wide. If that wasn't enough, Pontiac routinely asked its graphic designers to stretch the cars in illustrated ads to make them look even

YOU GET THE SOLID QUALITY OF BODY BY FISHER.

Pontiac launches a trim traveler...able and stable on wide-track wheels

Come aboard a 1959 Pontiac and see why this rakish new automobile has been sailing away with the honors this year.

Wide-Track Wheel design has played no small part and only Pontiac has it. The wheels are five inches farther apart. This widens the stance, not the car. The center of gravity is lower; there's a greater stability. You're more secure and confident at the helm.

Anchored, or in action, she's a trim car. The Wide-Track Wheel design gives her a sleek, slender, harmonious appearance. She's bal-

anced, not top heavy like conventional "narrow gauge" cars.

She's a much discussed car, respected, admired and owned by a new smart set tuned to a different kind of automobile perspective. Even the editors of Motor Trend Magazine, a most discriminating group of automobile judges, have awarded Pontiac their Car of the Year trophy for 1959.

Your Pontiac dealer has several in port, shipshape and ready for you to take on a cruise this week. Give him a call.

Wide-Track Wheels; New Economy Engine, Too!
Wheels are moved out 5 inches for steadier stance, easier handling. New Tempest 420E engine gives V-8 muscle and pep on regular grade gasoline. No other car offers these two automotive advancements!

PONTIAC! America's Number ① Road Car!

PONTIAC MOTOR DIVISION • GENERAL MOTORS CORPORATION

3 Totally New Series • Catalina • Star Chief • Bonneville

"See, I told you Pontiac was the CAR OF THE YEAR!"

"These guys at Motor Trend really know what they're talking about. They test all the new cars. Just like I've been saying, any car that looks as sharp as the new Pontiac, 'moves' like it does, and is such a 'ball' to drive, is bound to be something special."

The selection of the 1959 Pontiac as CAR OF THE YEAR, by Motor Trend Magazine came as no surprise to those who *really know* cars. As the editors said, "Pontiac with Wide-Track Wheels is the best combination of ride, handling, performance and styling of any '59 car."

Pontiac is as much at home at the drive-in as it is at the country club. Whether it's a stick shift

Catalina Coupe, with Tri-Power (three two-barrel carbs) or a Bonneville Vista with the new Tempest 420E economy engine, Pontiac is ready to show new pride and new performance unavailable in any other car.

And every Pontiac is built to handle this great performance. Its Wide-Track Wheel design moves the wheels five (5) inches farther apart for better balance and stability. This widens the stance, not the car. Gives it a safer, steadier grip on the road that no narrow track car can match.

Stop by your nearest authorized Pontiac dealer soon and put this great new car through its paces.

PONTIAC! America's Number ① Road Car!

PONTIAC MOTOR DIVISION • GENERAL MOTORS CORPORATION

Legendary automotive artists Art Fitzpatrick and Van Kaufman helped define Pontiac's new look beginning in 1959 with advertising illustrations, like the one on the left, that showcased the new split-grille and Wide Track wheels On the right, the '59 held bragging rights as *Motor Trend's* car of the year. **Opposite page:** Pontiac pulled out all the stops to draw attention to the '59's via direct promotional tie-ins with General Mills Cereals. Ads courtesy of the Automotive History Preservation Society.

wider. Visually, it made the car's front end look almost as wide as the road it was on.

But as wide a statement as the front grille made, the really big news in 1959 was the advent of Pontiac's signature "Wide Track" stance. The '59 models were lower and sleeker than their predecessors, and they sat atop the industry's widest wheel stance. This was more than just Madison Avenue hype. Pontiac pushed the wheels on its '59 models further out toward the fenders than anyone else – a full five inches over the 1958 model – to create what were considered the best-cornering full-size cars in the industry. The rest was history as Wide Track became a hallmark of Pontiac cars for years to come.

A recent story in Hemmings recounted how the final design actually came about:

"For General Manager Semon "Bunkie" Knudsen, this would be the first Pontiac line fully developed under his supervision since he arrived in the summer of 1956 with a plan to revitalize the division's models through youthful styling and increased performance. During a Saturday morning walk-around of the '59's clay model in the styling section with Chief Engineer Pete Estes, the Wide-Track concept was born. Knudsen shared the story with me for a 1994 interview for *High Performance Pontiac* magazine.

'"At that time, although the body styling was very appealing with the normal tread, the new Pontiac looked like a football player in ballet shoes,' Knudsen recalled. 'Pete and I moved the wheels out as a styling measure and it looked fantastic. We checked it out and found that the cost to make the change was minimal, so we went ahead and it was well worth it.'"

The new look presented the appearance of a crouching animal and sent Pontiac sales skyrocketing, from 319,719 in 1957 to 877,382 in 1968. But the 1959 Pontiacs – the first all-Knudsen models – were a turning point for the division, which quickly rose to third place in industry sales behind Chevrolet and Ford.

Pontiac's marketing machine ushered in the Bonneville with "Strato-Star" styling by touting its lower, longer body, split grilles, twin-fin rear fenders and, on non-convertible models, a 40 percent increase in glass area due to a huge front windshield and flat-top roofs on the Vista pillarless sedans.

In a 2010 feature, *Automobile Magazine* took note of Pontiac's big design advances in 1959, including a new front grille: "Two significant design innovations that have become associated with the Pontiac brand were introduced with the 1959 Pontiac Bonneville. Now in its third year, the Bonneville added a Vista sedan and Safari station wagon to its coupe and convertible lineup."

The 1959 Bonneville was marketed as a sporty luxury car, aimed at men who wanted a little fun behind the wheel. The Safari wagon focused on homemakers who needed a car to transport the kids. Though standard features were minimal, a host of options were available.

Inside, carpeted doors and walnut trim projected the image of rich, lush luxury. Leather seats were standard on the convertible, while vinyl came with all other trims. Six horsepower options were available with the 370 block V8 engine, ranging from 255 to 330, and depended on whether it had a four-barrel or TriPower carb. Only a 4-speed Hydramatic auto transmission was offered.

Indeed, the 1959 Bonneville was the most expensive car in Pontiac's stable. And with twin grilles up front, Bonneville owners considered it money well spent.

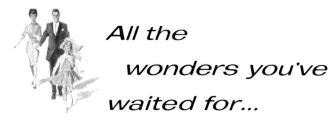

All the wonders you've waited for...

PONTIAC '59

GRILLE TECH SHEET: 1959 Pontiac Bonneville
Manufacturer: Pontiac Division, General Motors Corp.
Body by: Fisher Body Division, General Motors
Assembly Points:
    Pontiac, MI
    Flint, MI
    Ypsilanti, MI
    Wentzville, Mo
1959 model production: A total of 11,426 top-of-the-line Bonneville convertibles were produced in 1959.
    38,696 examples of the 4-door Vista Hardtop and 27,769 were 2-door hardtops.

Body Options
- 2-door convertible
- 2-door coupe
- 4-door station wagon
- 4-door hardtop

Engine: 389-cubic inch V-8 300HP @ 4400RPM, 420 ft. lbs. Torque @ 2800 RPM with standard equipment 4BBL Carb/Hydramatic
> **Fuel injection system and Tri-Power options available"
> Transmission: Automatic: 4-speed "Super" Hydramatic.
> **3-speed manual was available but not all models**

Wheelbase: All models except Bonneville Safari 124 inches
> Bonneville Safari 122 inches

Curb Weight: Convertible 4140 lbs/2dr HT 4170 lbs/Safari 4540 lbs/ 4dr HT 4140 lbs

MSRP:
> Base: In 2019 Dollars
> 2-Door HT $3,257 $30,257
> 4-Door HT $3,300 $29,115.30
> Safari Wagon $3,532 $30,853.66
> Convertible $3,478 $30,381

Current Values from Hagerty

- 2-door hardtop   #1 $58,700/#2 $42,100/#3 $23,200/#4 $10,600
- 2-door convertible #1 $91,200/#2 $66,500/#3 $37,200/#4 $26,400
- 4-door hardtop   #1 $31,200/#2 $20,200/#3 $11,600/#4 $6,500
- 4-ddor station wagon #1 $27,200/#2 $19,400/#3 $10,700/#4 $6,600

Below: North of the border, wide track and twin grills were big selling on the 1959 Parisienne.

All the finger-tip precision of a jet cockpit is yours in the '59 instrument panel. Instruments and appointments are grouped in circles and hooded for extra safety along the recessed panel. The Parisienne panel features a padded passenger assist rail mounted on the dash.

Here they are! And how you'll love their luxury . . . the low silhouette Pontiac Parisienne models for 1959. New in personality, new in power and performance, new in handling ease and road-hugging stability, the Parisienne Series brings you truly fine cars . . . but at popular prices.

All the luxury you've longed for . . . **PARISIENNE!**

PARISIENNE CONVERTIBLE

1959 Pontiac Colors

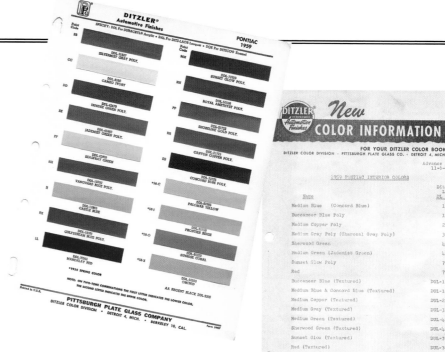

Paint Code

BB	DDL-31827 SILVERMIST GRAY POLY.
CC	DDL-8160 CAMEO IVORY
DD	DDL-42479 DUNDEE GREEN POLY.
EE	DDL-42480 JADEMIST GREEN POLY.
FF	DDL-42499 SEASPRAY GREEN
HH	DDL-12002 VANGUARD BLUE POLY.
JJ	DDL-12003 CASTLE BLUE
KK	DDL-12001 GULFSTREAM BLUE POLY.
LL	DDL-70961 MANDALAY RED

Paint Code

MM	DDL-70959 SUNSET GLOW POLY.
NN	DDL-50536 ROYAL AMETHYST POLY.
PP	DDL-21722 SHORELINE GOLD POLY.
RR	DDL-21723 CANYON COPPER POLY.
SS	DDL-12025 CONCORD BLUE POLY.
*58-C	DDL-80986 PALOMAR YELLOW
*58-I	DDL-21710 FRONTIER BEIGE
*58-O	DDL-60323 SUNRISE CORAL
*58-X	DDL-50503 ORCHID
AA	DDL-9300 REGENT BLACK (NO SWATCH)

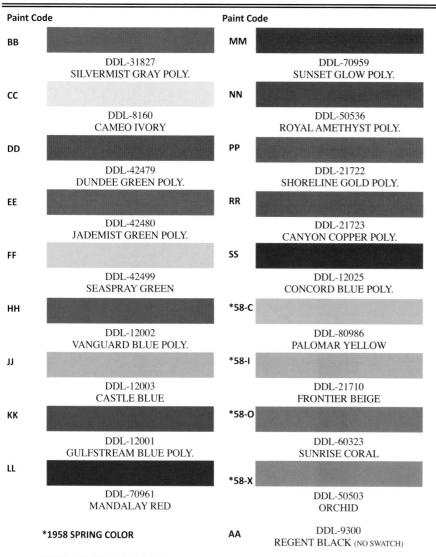

*1958 SPRING COLOR

NOTE: ON TWO-TONE COMBINATIONS THE FIRST LETTER INDICATES THE LOWER COLOR, THE SECOND LETTER INDICATES THE UPPER COLOR.

DITZLER COLOR DIVISION
PITTSBURGH PLATE GLASS COMPANY
Detroit 4, Michigan
Form 5907

SPECIFY { DDL – For DURACRYL Acrylic Lacqure
DAL– For DITZ-LAC® Automotive Lacquer
DQE– For DITZCO® Quickset Enamel

(Recreated for this publication for space and readability.)

New Color Information - Advance Bulletin 11-5-58

1959 PONTIAC INTERIOR COLORS
NEW COLOR

NAME	DITZLER CODE LACQUER DL/DAL
Medium Blue (Concord Blue	12025
Buccaneer Blue Poly.	12065
Medium Copper Poly.	21747
Medium Gray Poly. (Charcoal Gray Poly)	31876
Sherwood Green	42559
Medium Green (Jademist Green)	42560
Sunset Glow Poly.	70959
Red	71010
Buccaneer Blue (Textured)	DUL-12066
Medium Blue & Concord Blue (Textured)	DUL-12068
Medium Copper (Textured)	DUL-21746
Medium Gray (Textured)	DUL-31875
Medium Green (Textured)	DUL-42557
Sherwood Green (Textured)	DUL-42558
Sunset Glow (Textured)	DUL-70995
Red (Textured)	DUL-70996

2967-H
Red

2968-H
Coral Metallic

93075■
Dark Gray Metallic

93144■
Copper Metallic

93196■
Blue Metallic

93197■
Blue Metallic

93198■
Green Metallic

93199■
Green Metallic

93200■
Silver Metallic

"Duco Stock No.
or "Duco"
Formula File No.   Color

2967-H	Mandalay Red
2968-H	Sunset Glow metallic
93075■	Charcoal Gray Metallic
93144■	Samta Fe Copper Metallic
93196■	Buccaneer Blue Metallic
93197■	Concord Blue Metallic
93198■	Jademist Green Metallic
93199■	Sherwood Green Metallic
93200■	Starmist Silver Metallic

SPECIAL TEXTURED INTERIOR COLORS

2943-H	Santa Fe Copper Metallic
2944-H	Buccaneer Blue Metallic
2945-H	Concord Blue Metallic
2946-H	Jademist Green Metallic
2947-H	Sunset Glow Metallic
2949-H	Sherwood Green Metallic
2950-H	Charcoal Gray Metallic
2951-H	Mandalay Red

Note: There are no chips for special textured interior colors

1959 Pontiac interior colors

"Duco" Stock No.
or "Duco"
Formula File No.   PONTIAC

Color
2967-H   Mandalay Red
2968-H   Sunset Glow Metallic
93075■   Charcoal Gray Metallic
93144■   Santa Fe Copper Metallic
93196■   Buccaneer Blue Metallic
93197■   Concord Blue Metallic
93198■   Jademist Green Metallic
93199■   Sherwood Green Metallic
93200■   Starmist Silver Metallic

2967-H Red
2968-H Coral Metallic
93075■ Dark Gray Metallic
93144■ Copper Metallic
93196■ Blue Metallic
93197■ Blue Metallic
93198■ Green Metallic
93199■ Green Metallic
93200■ Silver Metallic

SPECIAL TEXTURED INTERIOR COLORS
2943-H   Santa Fe Copper Metallic
2944-H   Buccaneer Blue Metallic
2945-H   Concord Blue Metallic
2946-H   Jademist Green Metallic
2947-H   Sunset Glow Metallic
2949-H   Sherwood Green Metallic
2950-H   Charcoal Gray Metallic
2951-H   Mandalay Red

Note: there are no chips for special textured interior colors

STRATO-CHIEF 4-DOOR 6-PASSENGER SAFARI

Pontiac brings you four stunning new Safari station wagons for '59 . . .
all long on luxury and load space. Great workers by day,
Pontiac Safaris are equally at home in more formal company at night.
New this year is the luxurious Parisienne Safari, featuring
deep-pile carpets throughout, even on the load floor which has inlaid
metal skid strips for carpet protection and even easier loading.

PONTIAC SAFARI STATION WAGONS... *Practical pleasure for town and country*

PARISIENNE 4-DOOR 6-PASSENGER SAFARI

Fast Facts

Did you know?

- The 1959 Pontiac Bonneville was Pontiac's first step in a multi-year plan to rebrand the division as GM's sports performance leader.
- The new design propelled Pontiac into fourth place in domestic sales, ahead of both Buick and Oldsmobile.
- Bonnevilles were offered in four models. Besides the two-door coupe and convertible, Bonnevilles also came in a four-door hardtop version and a Custom Safari station wagon.
- Although all Pontiacs received new styling in 1959, the most significant in terms of promoting the brand's performance image was the Bonneville.
- Available as a two- or four-door hardtop, a station wagon and a convertible, the Bonneville stood apart from lesser Star Chiefs and Catalinas with special trim, more interior features (including a padded dash), and the brand's most powerful four-barrel and Tri-Power V-8s with up to 345 gross horsepower.
- The Bonneville's 64-inch wheel track – the widest in the industry at the time – was done in part to hide a styling flaw. The Bonneville's extremely broad body drooped awkwardly over the 1958-spec chassis. Pontiac head Bunkie Knudsen ordered the wheels pushed out to the edges for a more aggressive look.
- The new "Wide Track" look resonated with consumers. Sales for '59 increased by 76 percent (to 383,320), and the brand that was once considered an "old man's car" caught the attention of America's budding youth culture.
- The '59 Bonneville's formula was simple – stunning styling, V-8 muscle under the hood, and clever marketing (wider, longer, bigger, better). For Pontiac, they equaled greater exposure, sales and a new customer base.
- The '59 Bonneville can be seen in a number of '50s movies, including *Golden Gate* and *Strangers When We Met*. You can also catch a brief glimpse of a '59 Bonneville flat top in a *Leave it to Beaver episode*, and *Adam 12*.

Chapter 10:

1957 Cadillac Eldorado Brougham: *The Grille to End All Grilles*

The 1957 Cadillac Eldorado Brougham had a silky smooth 365-cubic-inch V-8 with two four-barrel carburetors that generated 325 horsepower. The same hefty V-8 in the 1958 model got three two-barrel carburetors for 335 horsepower. Power was fed through a four-speed Hydra-Matic automatic transmission. Cadillac publicity photo courtesy of The Automotive History Preservation Society.

There are some who believe the 1957 Cadillac Eldorado Brougham is the finest post-war Cadillac ever produced. Add to that claim the "priciest post-war Cadillac" and we would agree. There is little doubt that the '57 Eldorado Brougham was unmatched in design, detail, extravagance and price; a super luxury boulevard cruiser whose mere presence announced that you had arrived in the most expensive American luxury car on the market.

As with some of the other "Great Grille" cars in this book, the front grille of the '57 Eldorado Brougham isn't the only feature this Caddy is best remembered for. The eye-candy is virtually endless. Showroom shoppers were greeted with an amazing array of features that included:

- A brushed stainless-steel roof.
- Forged aluminum alloy/steel composite wheels.
- The world's first automotive air-spring suspension, which replaced traditional coil and leaf springs with air-filled bags that smoothed the ride and kept the car level under any load.
- Standard air conditioning.
- Separate front and rear heaters.
- A six-way power "memory" front seat.
- A two-speaker transistor radio, automatically latching electric door locks, Autronic Eye automatic headlamp dimming, polarized sun visors, power side and vent windows, a power trunk lid release, an electric clock, and more.
- A total of 44 full-leather interior and trim combinations, including Mouton, Karakul or lambskin carpeting.

As *Hemmings Motor News* noted in a 2008 feature: "Most unusual were the flagship's vanity items; pampered owners enjoyed a set of personal accessories that included a notepad with a silver Cross pencil, a plastic cigarette case holder, a color-coded ladies' compact and beveled glass hand mirror, a tissue dispenser, six magnetized-bottom drinking tumblers and, the pièce de résistance, a one-ounce atomizer of Arpège perfume from France."

Announced in December 1956 and released in March 1957, the Eldorado Brougham was a hand-built, limited production car derived from the Park Avenue and Orleans show cars of 1953–54. Designed by famed GM stylist Ed Glowacke, the Eldorado Brougham was priced at a little over $13,000, or the equivalent of more than $117,602 today. The price tag exceeded even the most expensive Rolls Royce of the day.

GM set out to build the finest luxury car of its time in response to Ford's all new ultra-chick Lincoln Mark II in 1956. The Eldo debuted to glowing reviews from the automotive press, which noted the car's opulence but also saw the Eldo as refined, technically advanced and incredibly good looking.

It's hard to believe the car was never a money maker. Cadillac reportedly lost $10,000 on each Eldorado Brougham made, as the market for ultra-luxury cars turned out to be softer than expected in 1957. But divisional heads never really expected it to be profitable. The car generated a ton of free publicity for Cadillac by enhancing the division's reputation for advanced engineering, and it drew plenty of prospective buyers of regular Cadillacs to showrooms. It also gave

GM set out to build the finest luxury car of its time – in response to Ford's all new ultra-chic Lincoln Mark II in 1956 – and the result was the 1957 Cadillac Eldorado Brougham. Cadillac publicists took advantage of every opportunity to spotlight the car's more prominent features. Dealer brochures, ads and publicity photos like the one on the left and on page 85 showcased the Eldorado's most prominent features – a dramatic cellular front grille, "projectile shaped gull-wing bumpers," the industry's first-ever quad (high- and low-beam) headlights, and rectangular fog lights. Cadillac visuals and promotional photos courtesy of the Automotive History Preservation Society and Antique Automobile Club of America.

future Cadillacs with the Eldorado name a reputation for unique styling and engineering advances that carried over to subsequent generations of front-wheel-drive Eldorados.

Only 400 were built in 1957 – not exactly what GM considered a mass production car – but enough ran off the assembly line to leave a lasting impression.

That includes the Eldorado's front grille assembly, which rightfully can lay claim to being among the car's most noticeable features. The grille is framed by a massive aluminum bumper that wrapped around the front fenders in tiers, creating a handle-bar moustache look. The chrome-plated curved cellular grilled is nestled between two staggering Dagmar nosecones, which Cadillac's PR team proudly described as "projectile-shaped gull-wing bumpers" with rubber insert tips "for safety."

Dagmars had been a standard feature on many Cadillacs throughout the 1950s. But, as with everything else on Cadillacs at the time, the '57's Dagmars were as big and ostentatious as they come. (For more on Dagmar bumpers and their origins, see Chapter 4.)

The entire grille assembly is flanked by a formidable bank of flood lights – above, on the driver and passenger side fenders, were four "quad" headlights featuring the first dedicated high- and low-beam illumination system on any American car. Below, on the grille's lower lip, are two rectangular fog lights. Sandwiched in between on each side of the grille are turn signal lights. Just in case that wasn't enough, Cadillac took pains to assure prospective buyers that the front end was complemented by the "smooth contour of the lower and flatter hood design."

The pitch worked on the rich and famous, who were among the first to place their orders. Frank Sinatra owned two '57 Eldorado Broughams. Elvis Presley, Bob Hope, Clark Gable, and Aristotle Onassis also bought them. One of Sinatra's cars sold at auction for $122,000 after his death. Today, the '57 Eldorado Brougham remains among the most desirable collector cars, with asking prices north of $200,000 for surviving models in top condition or celebrity pedigrees.

Just one piece of advice: If you pay top dollar, make sure yours comes with the six magnetized-bottom drinking tumblers in the glove box! And bring plenty of chrome polish for the grille.

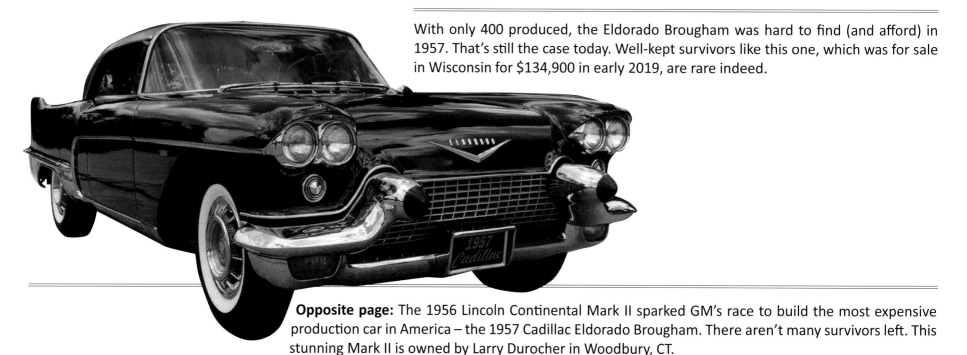

With only 400 produced, the Eldorado Brougham was hard to find (and afford) in 1957. That's still the case today. Well-kept survivors like this one, which was for sale in Wisconsin for $134,900 in early 2019, are rare indeed.

Opposite page: The 1956 Lincoln Continental Mark II sparked GM's race to build the most expensive production car in America – the 1957 Cadillac Eldorado Brougham. There aren't many survivors left. This stunning Mark II is owned by Larry Durocher in Woodbury, CT.

GRILLE TECH SHEET: 1957 Cadillac Eldorado Brougham

Manufacturer: Cadillac Division, General Motors

Body by: Fleetwood (Series 70)

Assembly Point: Detroit, MI

1959 Model Production: 400 hand-built units

Body: 4-door hardtop only

Engine: 365 cubic inches (6.0 L) overhead valve with dual 4-barrel Carter Carburetors. 325 horsepower, 400 ft. lbs. torque @ 3300 RPM

Transmission: 4 Speed Hydramatic Automatic

Rear Axle: 3.36:1

Overall Length: 216.3 Inches

Wheelbase: 126 Inches

Curb Weight: 5500 lbs. About the same as a mid-2000's Ford F-150 extended cab pickup with a V-8.

MSRP: $13,074 – In 2019 dollars, $118,271.78.

The MSRP for the Series 70 Eldorado Brougham was more than twice the price of any other Eldorado in 1957, and more than the 1957 Rolls Royce Silver Cloud.

Production Colors:

The Eldorado Brougham (as well as the Biarritz and Seville) had different color palettes than the other '57 Cadillacs. (No color palettes are available.)

Interior Colors: Cadillac offered buyers 44 choices of interior trim and color combinations when ordering. Several different leather and carpeting options were available as well.

Current Values from Hagerty

#1 $145,000/#2 $111,000/#3 $75,300/#4 $51,900

New Color Information - Advance Bulletin 5-28-57

1957 CADILLAC BROUGHAM COLORS
(DURACRYL–ACRYLIC)

PAINT CODE	NAME	DITZLER CODE LACQUER DL/DAL
110	Ebony	9200
112	Camonix White	8147
116	Wimbledon Gray Poly	31593
118	Deauville Gray Poly	31592
122	Lake Placid Blue Poly	11711
124	Copenhagen Blue Poly	11709
126	Fairfax Blue Poly	11710
132	Jamaican Green Poly	42180
134	Laurentian Green Poly	42179
136	Plantation Green Poly	42178
140	Manila	80945
144	Sandalwood	21476
148	Kenya Beige Poly	21477
149	Nairobi Maroon Poly	50497

MODELS – ELDORADO, BIARRITZ & SEVILLE
***(ACRYLIC DDL)**

90	*Olympic White	8144
92	* Starlight Poly	31530
94	*Bahama Blue Poly	11301
96	*Elysian Green Poly	42109
98	*Copper Poly	21417

1957 CADILLAC
COLOR CHANGE

Dusty Rose Poly, 70760 paint code 48, has been changed to 70788 paint code 48A. The name will remain the same.

A 1957 publicity photo of the all-new Eldorado Brougham.

A 1957 Cadillac Eldorado Brougham at a recent classic car show.

Fast Facts

Did you know?

- The 1957 Eldorado Brougham was derived from GM's flashy 1954 Park Avenue and 1955 Eldorado Brougham town cars, featured at GM's national Motorama auto shows.
- Not only did the Eldorado's quad headlights make it stand out in a crowded parking lot, they were also illegal in some states in 1957.
- We take for granted many of the power options that were standard on the '57 Eldorado Brougham today, but when it was introduced, power windows were almost as big a deal for consumers as owning a color TV.
- The Brougham's design was unique, over the top and, as one retrospective put it, "a flashy mix of Jet Age with a heavy swirl of Art Deco detailing."
- The Eldorado featured both front/rear center armrests. The rear one had a storage bin with note pad, pencil, mirror and a perfume atomizer stocked with Arpege, Extrait de Lanvin.
- The front seats were separate and independently adjustable, and they swung out. This created extremely wide and comfortable seating for two passengers, but made it quite uncomfortable for three. The front seats also included the first memory setting on any production car, as well as forged aluminum wheels.
- The Brougham's air suspension system – which many regard as its most innovative technological feature – proved unreliable, and Cadillac later released a kit to convert the cars to rear coil spring-type suspension.
- Another new technological feature on the Eldorado in 1957 was the ball joint suspension system.
- The new Eldorado was initially ignored by the automotive press – there are few reviews or test drives. Cadillac's introductory public relations effort didn't focus on preview publicity, and other models like the Fleetwood Sixty Special generated more media attention.
- It's easy to find the '57 Eldorado Brougham in movies such as *Ocean's Eleven* in 1960 and *Driving Miss Daisy* in 1989.

Opposite page: Move over Dan Tanna, the 1957 Ford Thunderbird's restyled front grille improved upon the original's design with a cleaner, more refined look that connected with buyers in record numbers. The '57s stood out as a luxurious alternative to the fledgling Corvette. This beauty is owned by Rick Dayton of Watertown, CT

Chapter 11:

1957 Ford Thunderbird: Ford Takes the Sports Car Challenge Personally

-1957-
Connecticut

Early American
Thunderbird

Produced from 1955-1957, the first-generation Ford Thunderbirds were instant classics. The sexy, sculptured lines of the first two-seaters are closely connected with the rise of American sports cars. Yet the T-Bird is often regarded as the more refined, more reliable steel-bodied competitor to Chevrolet's underpowered and often problematic Corvette, or foreign rivals like the MG, Triumph, Porsche and Jaguar.

But Ford never intended the T-Bird to be a sports car. Indeed, it was marketed as a "personal car," the first American personal luxury entry that would appeal directly to well-to-do buyers who wanted a fun drive without sacrificing comfort and great looks.

Purists at the time weren't impressed. But it didn't matter. The T-Bird immediately struck a responsive chord with consumers. Its understated and elegant front grille played a big role in the car's popularity (more on this later).

The T-Bird's styling, as was the case with many popular American cars of the 50s, was inspired in part by European designs.

The story goes that in 1952 Henry Ford II, the 35-year-old company chairman and grandson of founder Henry Ford, was becoming quite enamored with European sports cars. Enzo Ferrari gave him a Ferrari 212 Barchetta as a gift. At the time, the 212 was lighting up race tracks across Europe. At that year's Paris Motor Show, Ford took designer George Walker to task for not having something similar in the works. Walker promptly called his team in Detroit and told them to have a presentation ready when he returned from Paris.

The sports car project was quickly given the green light by Ford, and its development took on a new sense of urgency in January 1953, when Chevrolet released the Corvette. But Ford caught a break with the Corvette's teething problems. And when the first T-Bird debuted in 1955, it was everything the Corvette wasn't – roomier, more powerful, steel-bodied rather than temperamental fiberglass, and refined.

Nearly a year after the Corvette's launch, the Thunderbird premiered at the Detroit Auto Show. Not wanting to get trapped by journalists and owners who would complain about the car's less than stellar handling and speed, Ford promoted the car as a "sporty personal car." Defining it this way, the automotive press continued to laud the vehicle and millions of customers came to the showroom to see this exciting new vehicle from Ford.

Ford had only planned to build 10,000 T-Birds in 1955. But 10 days after it debuted in Detroit, Ford had over 3,500 orders. By the end of the model year, Ford sold more than 16,000 T-Birds at over $4,000 each when fully-loaded. That was no small feat, considering the Thunderbird could be twice as expensive as a base-model Ford coupe, and as much as the far more capable Jaguar XK140.

Another 15,600 cars sold for 1956. By 1957, the number jumped even higher to 21,300. By then, T-Birds could be ordered with manual or automatic transmissions and all the trappings of a luxury car that we take for granted today – power seats, a telescoping steering wheel and a removable hardtop, among others – and customers loved.

The 1957 Thunderbird sported a restyled appearance front and rear and was 6.1 inches longer than the '56 model to accommodate the spare wheel, which moved from an external mount on the back bumper back into the trunk. The longer, lower look of the '57 with carefully sculpted rear fins gave it a sleeker and more elegant appearance than its predecessors.

The front grille was enlarged to aid cooling, the lower front bumper was reshaped around the center grille, and then raised slightly on each end so as to not cover the T-Bird's gaping mouth. So even though the front fascia had a boxier appearance than previous T-Birds, the U-shaped bumper, with its rounded edges, gave the front of the car a softer and wider appearance.

The twin Dagmar bumper protectors (moderate in size compared to those at GM) that were stationed in front of the grilles on '55 and '56 models were incorporated into the lower bumper and repositioned so that they would not block the larger grille's appearance. It was a cleaner, less cluttered look.

The round-edged hood featured, as in previous models, a delicate scoop which gathers air through a polished grille. On either side of the grille, rectangular indicators were incorporated in the bumper which extends around the short front overhang and ends in line with the front wheel well. The twin-headlights setup was retained for 1957, as were the metal eyebrows of the two headlamps.

Among the many new features introduced in 1957 were 14-inch wire hubcaps hugged by whitewall tires. The rear wheels were covered by stylish covers with added chromed side skirts.

The front grille on early Ford Thunderbirds evolved from 1955-'57. The '55 and '56 models had smaller front grilles, moderate Dagmar bumper protectors, and slender single piece bumpers that were separate from the turn signals. The '57 sported an enlarged grille and a reshaped lower bumper that wrapped around the grille. The Dagmars were redesigned and incorporated into the lower bumper design. In this picture, a white '57 T-Bird, center, is flanked by a red '55 on the right and coral '56 on the left.

A new instrument panel from full-sized Fords had gauges nestled under a cowl, and options such as the Dial-O-Matic power seat which automatically went to a pre-set position when the car was started, automatic windshield washers, and a radio with volume that rose as engine speed increased.

While T-Bird fans love all of the original two-seaters, and many consider the '55 and '56 Birds to be the "purest" designs, the '57 Thunderbird is special. It was the last two-passenger Thunderbird before Ford decided big was better and transformed the T-Bird into a four-seater sports car with added amenities and weight. For many T-Bird fans, the '57 was a refinement over the original.

The '57 was the most powerful T-Bird, featuring for the first time a 5.1-liter V-8 engine, in a number of guises. Three-speed T-Birds carried a 292 cubic inch V-8, but others – like the rare and highly coveted "E-Birds" – held the 312 cubic inch engine rated at 245-285 horsepower. Supercharged 312's put out as much as 340 horsepower.

Only a few hundred E-Birds were built. They were equipped with twin quad-barrel carburetors and were distinguishable by the letter E in the car's VIN code, giving birth to the name "E-Bird." T-Bird historians will also note the development of the even rarer "F-Birds," a designation given to a handful of '57 Thunderbirds that featured a McCulloch supercharger on the 312 four-barrel V-8s. *Hemmings Motor News* called them "quite frankly, the pinnacle of the 1955-1957 two-seaters."

Generally recognized as "F-Birds" by virtue of the "F" engine identifier in the VIN, just 196 were built. All rolled off the assembly line after June 10 in the final stages of the 1957 model year.

The last two-seat Thunderbird was built on Dec. 13, 1957, and it was succeeded by the far better-selling (but to many, less collectible) four-seat "Square Bird;" 53,166 units were built in the car's first three years – proof positive that American consumers were embracing Detroit's "bigger, better" marketing mantra – a bet Ford actually made in 1955 because executives were concerned that two-seaters would not sell.

Yet it is hard to escape the reality that the first-generation 1955 to 1957 T-Birds were practically classics the moment they rolled out of the factory. The Thunderbird captured the attention and hearts of America and gave people a reason to go to Ford showrooms.

The Thunderbird launched a new market segment that would go on to dominate the American landscape within a few decades.

Today, the two-seat T-Birds embody the 1950s as much as a '59 Cadillac or a '57 Chevy. They remain among the most desirable cars of the 1950s, and their front grills are one of the era's most recognizable.

The '56 T-Bird's external spare tire mount disappeared in '57. Ford lengthened the truck and put the spare back inside.

GRILLE TECH SHEET: 1957 Ford Thunderbird
Manufacturer: Ford Motor Company, Dearborn MI
Body by: Ford
Assembly Point: Ford Assembly--Wixom, Michigan
1957 model production: 21,380
Body: 2-Door Convertible
Engine: CODE C 292 CUBIC INCH (4.7L)V-8, 212 HP 2BBL Carb
    Torque: 297 ft. lbs. @ 2700 rpm "Thunderbird V-8"
      CODE D 312 CUBIC INCH (5.1L) V-8, 245 HP 4BBL Carb
    Torque: 332 ft. lbs @ 3200 rpm "Thunderbird Special V-8"
      CODE E 312 CUBIC INCH (5.1L) V-8, 270 HP 2x4BBL Carb
    Torque: 336 ft. lbs. @ 3400 rpm "Thunderbird Super V-8"
      CODE E 312 CUBIC INCH (5.1L) V-8, 285 HP 2x4BBL Carb
    Torque: 343 ft. lbs. @ 3500 rpm "Thunderbird Super V-8 Racing Kit Edition"
      CODE F 312 CUBIC INCH (5.1L) V-8, 300 HP 4BBL Carb w/McCulloch Variable Ratio Centrifugal Supercharger
    Torque: 340 ft. lbs. @ 5300 rpm "Thunderbird Special Supercharged V-8"
    Note: All carburetors supplied by Holley Performance Products

Transmission: Standard: 3-speed Synchromesh with helical gears
Ratios: 2.32:1 (first); 1.48:1 (second); 1:1 (third); 2.82:1 (reverse)
Optional Overdrive: Planetary overdrive with planetary gears
Ratio: 0.70:1
Cut-In Speed: 27 mph
Cut-Out Speed: 21 mph
Optional Automatic: Ford-O-Matic torque converter with planetary gears
Ratios: 1.48:1 (drive); 2.44:1 (low); 2.0:1 (reverse)

Rear Axle:
    3.56:1 (Conventional)
    3:70:1 (Overdrive)
    3.10:1 (Ford-O-Matic)

Wheelbase: 102 Inches
Curb Weight: 3134 lbs.
MSRP: $ 2944 ($26,773 in 2019 Dollars)

Current Values from Hagerty:
With 292 CUBIC INCH Engine:
    #1 $81,600/#2 $57,200/#3 $37,900/ #4 $ 21,500
With 312 C.I 245 HORSEPOWER Engine:
    #1 $97,900/#2 $69,400/#3 $48,200/#4 $28,500
With 312 CUBIC INCH 270 HORSEPOWER 2x 4 BBL Engine:
    #1 $150,000/#2 $97,000/#3 $56,000/#4 $34,900
With 312 CUBIC INCH 300 HORSEPOWER Supercharged Engine: #1 $220,000/ #2 $155,000/ #3 $100,000/ #4 $62,400

1957 Ford Colors

Paint Code		Paint Code	

E — DQE-8103-DAL COLONIAL WHITE

F — DQE-11547-DAL STARMIST BLUE

L — DQE-21331-DAL DOESKIN TAN

K — DQE-21376-DAL SILVER MOCHA POLY.

T — DQE-31415-DAL WOODSMOKE GRAY

J — DQE-42025-DAL WILLOW GREEN

V — DQE-70707-DAL FLAME RED

Y — DQE-80859-DAL INCA GOLD

C — DQE-11602-DAL DRESDEN BLUE

N — DQE-31464-DAL GUNMETAL GRAY POLY.

G — DQE-42027-DAL CUMBERLAND GREEN

Z — DQE-70708-DAL CORAL SAND

*Q — DQE-50469-DAL THUNDERBIRD BROZE POLY.

*X — DQE-50470-DAL THUNDERBIRD DUSK ROSE

★W — DQE-41980-DAL SPRINGMIST GREEN

★Y — DQE-70706-DAL SUNSET CORAL

★V — DQE-41979-DAL BERKSHIRE GREEN

A — DQE-9000-DAL RAVEN BLACK (NO SWATCH)

*Thunderbird Color Only
★1956 Spring Color

LATE PRODUCTION (1958) COLORS

G - Sun Gold*+ (80948—Replaced Y - Inca Gold)

H - Gunmetal Gray*+ (3157 Replaced N - Gunmetal Gray)

L - Azure Blue*+ (11692—Replaced F - Starmist Blue)

N - Seaspray Green*+ (42171—Replaced J - Willow Green)

R - Torch Red*+ (70801—Replaced V - Flame Red)

Note:

IN COLOR COMBINATIONS THE FIRST LETTER INDICATES LOWER COLOR,
THE SECOND GENERALLY UPPER OR MIDDLE COLOR –
FOR EXAMPLE:

CONVENTIONAL TWO-TONES

A-E   LOWER RAVEN BLACK. 9000
       UPPER COLONIAL WHITE, 8103

STYLE TONES

A-E   LOWER RAVEN BLACK, 9000
       MIDDLE COLONIAL WHITE, 8103
       ROOF RAVEN BLACK, 9000

A-E   LOWER   RAVEN BLACK, 9000
       ROOF DECK & QRT
       IN. MIDG AREA   } COLONIAL WHITE, 8103

DITZLER COLOR DIVISION
PITTSBURGH PLATE GLASS COMPANY
Detroit 4, Michigan
Form 5709

SPECIFY { DAL– For DITZ-LAC® Automotive Lacquer
         { DQE– For DITZCO® Quickset Enamel

(Recreated for this publication for space and readability.)

Note: Because the 1958 Thunderbirds weren't ready for production in time to be introduced with the rest of the new Ford models, the company decided to hold over production of the 1957 models longer than usual to keep new Thunderbirds in dealer inventory. When the changeover to the 1958 models occurred at the factory, new 1958 colors were sprayed on the '57 T-birds to prevent any delays on the assembly line.

TU-TONE COLORS (EARLY PRODUCTION)
BODY CODE/TOP CODE - COLORS
AE - Raven Black/Colonial White
AF - Raven Black/Starmist Blue
AJ - Raven Black/Willow Green
AV - Raven Black/Flame Red
AX - Raven Black/Dusk Rose
AY - Raven Black/Inca Gold
AZ - Raven Black/Coral Sand
EA - Colonial White/Raven Black
EF - Colonial White/Starmist Blue
EN - Colonial White/Gunmetal Gray
EQ - Colonial White/Thunderbird Bronze
EU - Colonial White/Willow Green
EV - Colonial White/Flame Red
EX - Colonial White/Dusk Rose
EY - Colonial White/Inca Gold
EZ - Colonial White/Coral Sand
FA - Starmist Blue/Raven Black
FE - Starmist Blue/Colonial White

TWO TONE COLORS (LATE PRODUCTION)
BODY CODE/TOP CODE - COLORS
JA - Willow Green/Raven Black
JE - Willow Green/Colonial White
NA - Gunmetal Gray/Raven Black
NE - Gunmetal Gray/Colonial White
NY - Gunmetal Gray/Inca Gold
QE - Thunderbird Bronze/Colonial White
VA - Flame Red/Raven Black
VE - Flame Red/Colonial White
YA - Inca Gold/Raven Black
YE - Inca Gold/Colonial White
YN - Inca Gold/Gunmetal Gray
XA - Dusk Rose/Raven Black
XE - Dusk Rose/Colonial White
ZA - Coral Sand/Raven Black
ZE - Coral Sand/Colonial White
ZN - Coral Sand/Gunmetal Gray
Note: 1958 colors (noted above) were used from September-December 1957.

Interior Colors:
TRIM CODE - COLOR (BOLSTER/PLEATED SECTIONS)
XA - Black/White
XH - Red*
XJ - Copper*
XK - White*
XL - Medium Blue/Light Blue*
XM - Medium Green/Light Green* (shown at left)

HEADLINER
White perforated vinyl

CONVERTIBLE TOP
Black Rayon   White Vinyl
Blue Rayon*   Tan Rayon*

The popular roof top port hole remained a signature styling feature on the '57 T-Bird

Fast Facts

Did you know?

- First generation Thunderbirds are true movie and TV stars. Perhaps the most memorable is the white 1956 T-Bird driven by Suzanne Somers in *American Graffiti*.

- Interest in the '57 T-Bird skyrocketed in the 1970s when the car was featured in the popular ABC-TV series *Vega$* starring Robert Urich. Two identical red T-Birds were used on the show, one for close-ups and beauty shots, and the other as a stunt car for chase scenes and an occasional off-road desert romp. The Thunderbird was so popular that during a talk show interview Urich commented, "That car got more fan mail than I did!"

- The 1957 T-Bird has appeared in dozens of movies including *Pal Joey* with Frank Sinatra, *The Thrill of It All*, starring Doris Day and James Garner (where he drove a 1958 Chevy Bel Air into the family's backyard swimming pool), *Indiana Jones and the Kingdom of the Crystal Skull*, and *The Lords of Flatbush*, among many others.

- In addition to television shows, movies and print advertisements, the first-generation Thunderbirds were pictured on a U.S. postage stamp in 2005.

- Almost from the day it went on sale, the two-seat Thunderbird was hailed as a classic. By the mid-1960s, they were becoming treasured vehicles when other models from the same era were considered old cars.

- The 1957 Thunderbird was the last two-seater Ford sold until the 1982 Ford EXP sport compact car.

- "Ford boasted that the T-Bird had outsold all other sports-type personal cars combined. According to *Popular Mechanic's 1957 Car Facts Book*, the 1956 model, outsold its principal domestic competitor, the Chevrolet Corvette, by more than 10 to 1. Even though the Corvette had whipped the T-Bird in sports car racing, the T-Bird was the big winner on the boulevards of America," *Old Car Reports.*

- The 1957 T-Bird was a favorite of celebrities. Burt Reynolds, who is best known for the Pontiac Trans Am he drove in *Smokey and the Bandit*, drove one. Pictures of Marilyn Monroe's T-Bird are everywhere, except hers was a 1956 model. Frank Sinatra also owned a '56. Singer Barbra Streisand owned one. Mel Blanc, the voice of Bugs Bunny and many other cartoon characters, also owned a rare supercharged F-Bird.

- A wide selection of colors was offered for the 1957 T-Bird. While single-tone editions were quite popular, many were available in a two-tone combination with the removable hardtop receiving a contrasting hue.

- '57 T-Birds equipped with a Paxton-McCulloch supercharger and 312 cubic inch V8 are very rare. The blower cost $500 ($4,556.80 in today's dollars) and added a 6 psi boost. Only 208 blown T-Birds were produced (13 for NASCAR racing) and they were capable of going from 0-60 mph in under seven seconds.

Authors

Mark Misercola is a writer, author, and classic car collector who has a passion for American cars from the 1950s and '60s. Mark started his career as a journalist covering the automobile industry for the Buffalo (N.Y.) *Courier-Express*. *Today*, his regular commentaries on collector cars can be found online in his blog (*REO Speed Blog*).

Mark grew up in an Oldsmobile family ("some men are Baptists...others Catholics ...my father was an Oldsmobile man"). Today, he owns two 1960 Oldsmobiles (including a four-door Super 88 that is nearly identical to his father's Oldsmobile) and a 1966 Oldsmobile Toronado. His bucket list includes a 1955 and 1957 Oldsmobile.

His first novel, *Death to the Centurion*, was published in 2001 by Twilight Times Books. He has also ghost written several management books, including *Silent Sabotage* and *Total Career Fitness* with William J. Morin, the retired CEO of Drake Beam Morin, and a pioneer in career counseling. Mr. Misercola works in Public Relations in New York.

Hank Kaczmarek is a classic car collector and one of the nation's leading technical experts on American cars built during Detroit's golden era. Give him a year, a make and a model, and he will tell you a story, as well as the specifications and part numbers.

Hank became a car nut/gear head at a young age and has never looked back. In high school, he could often be found reading *HOT ROD* magazine in the library instead of attending class.

Always fascinated by the Corvair, Hank has restored and owns several vintage Corvairs. He found his first Corvair in a junk yard in 1987 and bought it for $250. Since then he has owned and restored over a dozen Corvairs and has served as a national officer in the Corvair Society of America. He was a contributing writer to *Corvair Basics (An Intro to the Unique Technical and Mechanical Aspects of 1960-1969 Corvair)* in 2000. Hank worked in the auto sales and parts business for more than 20 years, including seven years as a product specialist for Steele Rubber Products.

Index